The Long Way Home

LORRAINE ADAMSON

WESTBOW®
PRESS
A DIVISION OF THOMAS NELSON
& ZONDERVAN

Copyright © 2015 Lorraine Adamson.

All rights reserved. No part of this book may be used or reproduced by any means, graphic, electronic, or mechanical, including photocopying, recording, taping or by any information storage retrieval system without the written permission of the publisher except in the case of brief quotations embodied in critical articles and reviews.

This book is a work of non-fiction. Unless otherwise noted, the author and the publisher make no explicit guarantees as to the accuracy of the information contained in this book and in some cases, names of people and places have been altered to protect their privacy.

Scripture taken from the Holy Bible, NEW INTERNATIONAL VERSION®. Copyright © 1973, 1978, 1984, 2011 by Biblica, Inc. All rights reserved worldwide. Used by permission. NEW INTERNATIONAL VERSION® and NIV® are registered trademarks of Biblica, Inc. Use of either trademark for the offering of goods or services requires the prior written consent of Biblica US, Inc.

WestBow Press books may be ordered through booksellers or by contacting:

WestBow Press
A Division of Thomas Nelson & Zondervan
1663 Liberty Drive
Bloomington, IN 47403
www.westbowpress.com
1 (866) 928-1240

Because of the dynamic nature of the Internet, any web addresses or links contained in this book may have changed since publication and may no longer be valid. The views expressed in this work are solely those of the author and do not necessarily reflect the views of the publisher, and the publisher hereby disclaims any responsibility for them.

Any people depicted in stock imagery provided by Thinkstock are models, and such images are being used for illustrative purposes only. Certain stock imagery © Thinkstock.

ISBN: 978-1-4908-8449-3 (sc)
ISBN: 978-1-4908-8451-6 (hc)
ISBN: 978-1-4908-8450-9 (e)

Library of Congress Control Number: 2015909432

Print information available on the last page.

WestBow Press rev. date: 6/25/2015

This is for my families, blood and spiritual,
and friends and neighbors, old and new.
Thank You, dear Father, for all the good gifts.

INTRODUCTION

This is a true story.

It had to be: that was an edict handed down by God—yes, *that* God, the Supreme Authority, the Creator of heaven and earth and everything else. The God of 'Thou shall not bear false witness'.

Let us hope the gift of storytelling came along with the compulsion to tell the truth.

I'm at a point where I finally *can* write—I have the time. I've *made* the time. And I'm invisible, which gives me a real edge when it comes to keeping an objective eye on people and situations. Does invisibility provide an objective lens for looking up and down time? We'll see. Or maybe we won't...

I don't mean that I'm literally invisible; but I am a middle-aged single woman, which practically equals invisible.

That sounds cynical, but it's merely an observation. I've reached the age, and more to the point, I *look* like I've reached the age, where I can only be a middle-aged mom or a potential purse-snatchee. I'm certainly not frail, but my hair is greying to white, and no matter what I do to it from now on, it's not going to look natural in any color unrelated to grey or white. People—*relevant* people (young, hip people)—tend not to notice my demographic. That gives me a freedom which, in my opinion, quite compensates for the sting of invisibility.

What's ironic is that those who *can* still see me have somehow gotten the idea that I'm 'cool'.

It's partly the glasses: they're far too trendy. An idiot could don glasses like mine, and with the right clothes, look dauntingly intellectual and effortlessly cool. These are glasses that make you look smart even without a serious expression on your face. A serious expression and a judiciously closed mouth go a long way toward making a person look brainy. I should know.

As for the cool, the reason I've finally got it is that I don't really care about it anymore.

I figured out that a big part of being cool is simply not pretending to give a rip about stuff you actually don't give a rip about. It's incredibly freeing, and knowing you're free gives you a confidence that can't be bought. That's all cool is.

These are just observations. It's nice to be able to record observations.

'God places the lonely in families; He leads forth the prisoners with singing. Only the rebellious dwell in a parched land.'

That's from the bible, Psalm 68, verse 6. I read the bible now, and that's one of my favorite verses.

It resonated with me the first time I read it; it seemed to speak to me directly. I used to think it meant that once you were safely placed within a family you'd no longer be lonely. And that once you were freed from the imprisonment of your iniquity, you'd be singing for joy. Mostly I still believe that's what it means, but sometimes lately I wonder...

Because even though I'm in a family I'm still lonely sometimes. And while I do find myself singing for joy fairly regularly, I occasionally wonder if maybe I've been reading it wrong all this time, and that really it's *His singing* that leads forth the prisoners. Because even when you think you know

Him, He surprises you with inchoate longings still; so I find myself listening, head cocked, for some kind of divine Mister Tambourine Man, whose music will lead me inexorably away to freedom. God as the Pied Piper...

And why does it feel sometimes like I'm still wandering in the desert? In the midst of plenty and blessing, why do I sometimes feel like none of it could possibly be mine? Where's the rebellion that keeps me far from home?

Maybe I'm still dragging some chains around.

CHAPTER 1

So let me tell you about the family God placed me in.
First, Neil Diamond isn't really my father.

No kidding, right? But knowing that Neil Diamond isn't my father also meant knowing that my mother lived with a significant mental illness. How are you supposed to go back to the beginning and find your way once you've realized the map you've been following is not only illusory, it isn't even your own illusion?

And how do you cleanse that illusion from your burned and shell-shocked life without dishonoring the person who gave you such a beautiful and terrible gift? If she could read these words, would her dear heart break? Now that she's gone, how can I show her how tenderly I loved her, yet place her craziness far away from me, away from my damaged brother and sisters?

Because it *was* a beautiful gift: beautiful and poison, like Snow White's apple or Rip Van Winkle's mountain wine. It was a thing that seduced with its lush, sparkling beauty and heady promise, yet it blighted every blessing of the present.

What a time it was: The dawning of the New Age—and for her, freedom from the debauchery and claustrophobia of her old life. A moment of breathless anticipation as she realized she could have her own ideas and thoughts—that she could wander fearlessly for the first time. But she dreamed so deeply into the spirit woods that she could not find her way back. Certainly the beast she met there looked more like a savior than a psychosis. Why wouldn't she follow him? He seemed to know the way.

Sometimes I wonder at my complicity. Yes, I was just a kid—and not a very worldly one at that, a bit fey myself. But I have kids, and I don't believe they'd let me get away with living the kind of dream that I allowed my mother to live. Only once, timidly, did I try to nudge Mom back to hard-headed reality. It was springtime 1973, when the spell was just beginning to set, that I made some small remark to show I knew she was only kidding about Neil Diamond's presence in our lives—and the look she gave me was as piercing and direct as her words: "I've never been more serious." She didn't acknowledge the joke because it wasn't a joke—it was her reality. So I had to choose between following a lost soul, and not following anybody. I wasn't aware of another option. Not following anybody was what I was used to, and probably what I should have stuck with—but I was fourteen and it was a time of new beginnings. So I chose to follow.

After all I was finally wandering fearlessly, too. For the first time since age six I was at a school where nobody knew my name was Bucky Beaver, or worse, Fleabag. And my mom was turning out to be such a smiling, curious companion—an interesting somebody who was looking for her own stuff along the way. How could I help but get caught up in her odyssey? She was the mom; she was supposed to be leading us. When she got lost we coped by believing—or pretending to believe—that we weren't lost at all; we believed that we were blessedly on the less-travelled path, headed for the best of all possible homes.

We'd come from perhaps not the worst of all possible homes, but it was certainly not a place of comfort and refuge. We learned, in our home, that our security was shaky—our roof and sustenance were never to be taken for granted, because they might disappear any minute. By age nine or ten, I lied for my father regularly, telling creditors on the telephone that he wasn't home. One year, our new living room furniture was not to be mentioned to our kindly old landlady, because the rent was in arrears.

Home was where we learned to fear our unpredictable father, who could turn into a monster for no apparent reason. He was the man who called his child daughters filthy names in a way that, though we didn't understand the words, we knew they meant we disgusted him. He was the man who built a bonfire in our back yard and burned all of our toys, the dear stuffed creatures we'd loved since babyhood, Dakoo and Scottie and Yellow Kitty. I was maybe eight years old; Lou would have been six and George and Joanie only toddlers. It's a hazy memory, or maybe a smoky one: Lou and I, our own hearts mauled, trying to comfort the twins. Or maybe it was George and Joanie trying to comfort Lou and me as we got off the afternoon school bus. Did Dad burn their animals too, or just mine and Lou's, because we were older, old enough to be finally keeping our room tidy? There we were, the four of us: partners in grief. Hearts not yet old or hard enough to let those imaginary lives end in the great whoosh of sudden gasoline fire and black smoke in a rusty steel drum where our yard met the woods; we kept them alive for each other in heaven. One of the twins' animals, a small woolly lamb who escaped the inferno, hung on the clothesline camouflaged amid socks and towels, witness to that grubby little crime. (Do you remember?)

Dad was a man whose fear and sadness poisoned him to madness. He should have been Irish—his was the tragic, inevitable violence of a glimmer of poetry, a little education, poverty, and alcohol.

From Dad I learned at a tender age to hate Americans with a fierce and loyal loathing. My widowed paternal grandmother lived in Niagara Falls, only a few minutes' walk from the Rainbow Bridge between Ontario and New York State. Many Sunday afternoons were spent sitting stiffly at attention in her meticulously kept living room. On summer Sundays, we might play carefully in her back yard, though the term *back yard* hardly fit; her property was as smooth and weedless as a golf course. We didn't really play either; clean, brushed, and ironed as we were, we were hardly our usual rough-and-ready selves.

My grandmother Adamson's back yard was a shady, cool, and entirely private green oasis for sticky Ontario August, hemmed all around by mature oaks and maples, cloistered amid lush shrubbery, and bordered by elegant flowers who'd never deign to stray from their beds. She had neighbors, but you couldn't see their houses or their yards; she lived in an impenetrable green fortress. The long hill behind her house was perfect for rolling down, but there were no boisterous country-kid games played on Grandma Adamson's impeccable grass. My cousins, who lived there along with Dad's sister and brother-in-law, were two and four years older than me. They were city girls, as carefully groomed as Grandma Adamson's yard—I couldn't imagine either of them ever rolling down a hill. I loved my grandmother's big Edwardian house, and I loved her cool, long-shadowed lawn, but secretly I felt that both were wasted on my city relatives.

Touring helicopters and small planes joined the muted background roar of the nearby falls. It was the white noise of hot summer days, as constant and unchanging as Dad's long rage against American drivers.

Niagara Falls was my father's city, and the Niagara Parkway, especially where it wound its gracious way through Queen Victoria Park, was Dad's very own king's road. As far as he was concerned, the Americans that hindered his progress whenever he drove through the park were no better than children who left roller skates on stairs. In summer especially, the parkway teemed with tourists, nearly all Americans, who *drove* like tourists: very slowly, doing their best to take everything in–the horse-drawn buggies, the manicured Victorian primness of sunny gardens and park, the exotic and lovely Indian brides as bright as tropical flowers in their wedding saris, and of course the stunning raw power of the falls. Though he could have gone home another way, my father always opted for the drive through his park.

Dad's state developed fairly predictably. After leaving Grandma Adamson's he'd turn onto the Niagara Parkway at the bottom of Seneca Street, and head towards the falls and Queen Victoria Park. We'd drive along for a couple of minutes pointing out 'foreign' license plates—New York plates didn't count, they were far too common. But there were cars from Connecticut and Pennsylvania, New Jersey and Ohio. We kept a sharp eye open for vehicles from truly exotic places–Florida and Georgia, Oregon and California. Mom and Dad played this game along with Lou and me–the twins were still too young to read.

Just a minute or two after leaving Grandma Adamson's house, the road curved into the park, and traffic went from slow and steady to stop-and-go. Cars crawled along at a snail's pace as their drivers' sought parking spots, and Dad would start to make the little irritated tsks and huffs that meant he was beginning to heat up. With the noises came neck-snapping jolts as he shifted gears—down and down, back up for a few yards, down again as the parkway traffic hiccupped along. Then some unfortunate would dare to stop in front of him to wait while another vehicle left a parking spot, and Dad's mantra would begin: a long, low-voiced, comma-less growl of curses that ran the gamut from vulgar to obscene to profane. The intensity of his tirade increased in direct proportion to the volume of traffic. Only three non-curse words ever made it into his rant, and invariably those words were "stupid", "Yankee", and "idiot". By the time I was five or six, my heart burned with scorn whenever anybody mentioned Americans.

Dad had a way with words; it wasn't a good way. When we'd committed some childhood infraction, he'd sit like a terrible giant in his chair, and demand to know why, in a voice that always started fearful tears. Rendered witless with fear, mounting a defense was impossible. Admitting our sin was out of the question; the consequences were too dire. I could never face Dad in his judgement seat without crying, and once I'd begun to cry, his disdain for my weak character became apparent. "What are you blatting about?" he'd want to know. "Your bladder is too close to your eyes! Quit your blubbering or I'll give you something to blubber about!" We usually got the "something to blubber about" anyway, so those ugly words only made me cry harder, and it wasn't the clean weeping of repentance. There was awful ritual to Dad's discipline technique, a sense of inevitable doom—grace wasn't part of his parenting milieu. The moments that lead up to the actual 'spanking' were torture; being sent to get the belt out of the kitchen drawer, the short walk down the hall back to the bedroom as dreadful to my young imagination as a walk to the scaffold. You want to get the whole thing over as quickly as possible, but your feet drag.

CHAPTER 2

'And we know that in all things God works for the good of those who love Him, who have been called according to His purpose.'

That's another bible verse; Romans 8:28. I used to misremember that verse, to generalize it so that God works all things for good, period. It's hard to reconcile *that* with life, when you're blindsided by grief and tragedy, for instance. Just how are 'all things' being worked 'for the good'? But of course what it really says is that *in all things He works for the good of those who love Him, who have been called according to His purpose*. A very different promise...

As a kid I didn't know much about God; I didn't get enough formal teaching to result in even the shakiest theology. Occasionally an aunt talked my parents into accompanying her to church, but we rarely attended longer than a month at a time, and then we might not go again for a year or more. We were hardly even Christmas & Easter churchgoers. I went to Sunday school around Christmastime once as a young child, and the class was asked to model a nativity scene out of Plasticine. My five and six year old classmates all worked diligently at little mangers and Marys and baby Jesuses. Enthusiastically, I rolled at my lump of clay. Plasticine was something I knew—we used it at school, and I was an expert. Soon I had a fine snake to share with the class.

The teacher gave me an irritated look. "We aren't doing Adam and Eve," she said.

Maybe she prayed for me.

Dad sang hymns. He had grown up in the cloistered and dusty Anglican tradition, a choirboy who knew all about the hypocrisy of the church long before the dissipation of the priesthood was common knowledge. I still remember the words to "Bringing in the Sheaves", even though I haven't heard it for more than 40 years. That memory is so old that it's attached to an image of Heaven as a rural washday, with all God's children rejoicing as they bring the sheets in off the line. God Himself was vaguely characterized as a grandfatherly overseer, watching benevolently from his great rocking-chair throne on the veranda of an enormous mountainside palace as His people gathered fresh linen from a clothesline stretched between summits. He seemed to greatly approve of the work they did, which struck me as a bit eccentric. Sweet, but kind of funny... Privately I thought God might need some looking after Himself, if He was that easily pleased. ("What?! Help with the laundry? Is *that* all You want?") My mother expected more of me.

It didn't occur to me to question those lyrics; just as it never occurred to me to ask what a 'shusquean' was, or why the grey one was in particular need of salvation. I remember feeling that I was participating in something important from the world of grown-ups as I stood at attention beside my grade one desk and sang those solemn words along with the rest of my class: "God save our grey shusquean..." You are a kid: you don't ask.

Another childhood notion was that Jesus had a wooden arm, a misconception also engendered by my dad. He used to sing "Leaning on the Everlasting Arm" as I hung over the ornately carved wooden arm of a tapestry chair that stood beside a little

Hammond organ in our living room. And Dad told me I could lean on Jesus' arm, just like I was leaning on that chair, and that it was so strong it would never get tired or break.

Seeds dropped by my earthly dad, then just a casual believer—perhaps not casually, but without an inkling of their ultimate power and significance. Dad could not have known those seeds would wait for decades, latent, on soil not yet ready to support their germination. He could not have known the disappointments and despair that would finally drive his daughter to look outside of herself for hope.

He wasn't a monster then, just a young dad trying to put a big truth into a little girl's heart. You could even say he was a noble young dad. That he obeyed that particular urge seems bewildering in light of his later dissolution.

It amazes me that I have these memories—I'd have been under six, not yet in school.

We used to play house outdoors with our dolls sometimes, my sister Lou and I, using a beat-up old 1950's change table as our kitchen. It was chrome and vinyl, like all the practical accoutrements of that era, the padded shelf sprinkled with pale turquoise dots and gold, long-rayed stars. 'House' was baking and doing laundry. Mom gave us a mixing bowl filled with dish soap and a little water, and an old-fashioned egg beater for making sudsy 'icing'. We did doll laundry with the garden hose. Lou's Bunny Esmond blanket was the only thing good enough for her doll baby Timothy. The blanket was a gift from our Grandma—Mom's mother—around the time the twins were born. Lou and I rarely played with dolls—we were both tomboys; but I remember Marjory, who was Grandma's gift to me, named after Grandma's sister because of her long, rich auburn hair. Those were the days Lou was nicknamed 'Crosspatch' by Mom, and I was her

'Calamity Jane'. Grandma was full of endearments, too: I was 'Dolly'; Lou was 'Ducky'.

Sometimes in southern Ontario, a summer rain came down so hard and warm that Lou and I could shower and wash our hair in the driveway. There wasn't a shower in our little country house bathroom, so that was an exotic treat for us.

There's stuff back there—back then—that I wonder about. I wonder what became of all the dishes and pots and pans after Mom packed us up and left. Homely little household items like the cream yellow plates with the brown oak-leaf-and-acorns border, and Mom's three-legged colander. Why do I remember them? For years I held a different colander in secret judgment because it wasn't made of aluminum, and didn't have three little feet.

I wonder how I got the scar on my right thigh. It looks like a vaccination mark just above my knee, and it's always been there. I asked Mom once, and she said "Ask your father". I never got an answer. Maybe now I'll never know.

And I wonder what happened to Napper. I know Dad shot him, after he'd gotten into the new neighbor's garbage a third or fourth time. He was a year or two older than me then, 13 or 14, an old dog. A *good* old dog. Dad loved him at least as much as I did, and Napper was like a big brother to me. So what happened? Did the new neighbor, with his raw new house planted arrogantly on what used to be our toboggan hill, make a stink and complain about our good old country dog running loose? Did he threaten to sic some bylaw officer on us? I only know coming home from school one day, grade six, and asking "Where's Napper?" because Napper was just about the only good thing in my life by then, utterly reliable, unconditionally loving, unashamedly glad to see me get off the school bus every day. "Where's Napper?" because he wasn't there.

Did Dad shoot him because he couldn't bear the thought of poor old Napper tied up? By then he had rheumatism and grey hair in his muzzle, and he got up creakily. He wasn't an indoor dog—didn't Dad think he could survive another winter in our unheated garage? I wonder what went through his head as he led Napper away... (Where did it happen? I always imagine Dad taking him out to the woods, but then what? How do you put a gun against your good dog's old head and pull the trigger?)

I wanted to see him, but he was already gone for good. I never even found out where Dad buried him. Losing Napper was the beginning of the end of normalcy at our house. It wasn't long after Napper died that things began to get truly frightening. Or maybe it just seemed that way because he wasn't around for comfort and distraction.

How blessed I am, to feel the mild west-coast sun on my face, to walk outdoors for joy. September is here—September the beautiful, the bountiful, the capricious. Today was perfect for gathering the year's last good crop of Himalayan Cutleaf blackberries. I call them super-berries: they're firmer, sweeter, and bigger than their commoner cousins. Their leaves are more sharply serrated, they ripen later, and they're a lot thornier. Everything about them is superlative, hence the nickname 'super-berries.' Super-berries belong to the absolute gravity of September, to the moment when ripe is at its utmost, and the next moment begins the inevitable decline to decay.

A day like today is a sweet gift; thank You!

I watched as a heron took off across the lake while mist was still caught like cotton batting in the rushes. All tangled up with the year's burst cattails, it was hard to tell where cattail fluff ended and mist began. I saw little narrow pathways going off into the woods, into the long wet grass, paths that maybe led to secret sunlit meadows, or hidden pixie-sized doorways among the roots of guardian trees.

When you spend your gift of a day walking alone, is anything more appealing, more promising, than a bend in the road? What will I find? (What am I looking for?) Surely more than a novel vista—isn't there the expectation of someday, around some sun-dappled crook in the dusty road, meeting the Familiar Stranger? Of suddenly finding the home so long-lost that not even the memory of a memory remains, only the yearning, the knowing you'll recognize it when you see it again. Maybe heaven will be around a bend in the road.

That's what I hope. That's what I expect. I'll meet The Stranger. But of course, He won't be 'The Stranger' anymore, I'll recognize Him immediately, and after all He's known me since forever. We'll walk together around a bend in the road, and there will be home (Home) and maybe Dad will be there with Napper, and I'll finally get to ask him what really happened—not that it'll matter—and he'll be able to tell me. There won't be recrimination, or guilt, or broken-hearted tears, only understanding.

CHAPTER 3

Now that Mom is gone, I can have a conversation while a Neil Diamond song plays on the radio. It isn't easy, but I can do it. Even after all these years, it takes conscious effort to tune it out. (I still have a bunch of albums bought between 1977 and the mid-eighties. I can't seem to bring myself to get rid of them.) For years—decades!—I was compelled to listen, as though he really was my mother's star-crossed mate, and therefore something big to me, too. (My *good* father...) So that's another scab to pick. I didn't catch the whole psychosis, but I came down with a bad case of secondary delusion. It was very contagious.

Contagious, and as fraught with stigma as a venereal disease...

For some time I wandered dazed, as if in the aftermath of a terrible accident—there was that still moment after everything had settled, and the only sound was the buzzing in my brain. That was the shock of realizing, finally, that my mother was delusional, and that I had spent years lost in it, right beside her. And then the moment, years long, afraid to assess my condition in case there were mortal wounds. Sometimes it's still scary to look closely - maybe I'm scarred for life. Morbid curiosity makes me peek under the bandages to see how things are coming along—is there infection? Am I going to lose that part of my psyche? Will I have to keep it in quarantine forever? (Is it hereditary? Are my kids susceptible?)

Was it better for the siblings, or worse? They were younger, Lou eleven, the twins only seven when Neil Diamond became my mother's imaginary lover. The twins still half-believed in Santa—maybe it was just like having another Santa to believe in. But, unlike me, they had the sense not to talk about it at school, so maybe they suspected early on that there was something not quite normal about the whole thing. Can they be blamed for finding it difficult to buy into the concept of another Invisible Friend?

We've never talked about it, my brother and sisters and me. We've never talked together about how it was for us. Did it get into their lives as thoroughly as it did mine? Did any of them ever try to coax Mom away? Her mother did, once. But Mom's outlandish story frightened Grandma deeply, and that panic got in the way of any help she might have been able to offer.

Grandma was a woman who spoke truths with wonderfully pithy and practical words, but her down-home demeanour could never quite conceal the shimmer of a wild romantic. I cherish memories of sitting around her kitchen table after supper, before even the plates had been cleared, while she read *The Lady of Shallot*, or sang as much of *Danny Boy* as she was able before she had to give up, weeping. She had talent, too, somewhere to pour her joy and passion; she painted and wove tapestries, cooked and wrote poetry. Family stories told to her grandchildren became treasured heirlooms. She had outgrown most of her wildness by the time we knew her, but looking back, I see the family gift in her like a vein of exotic ore—something priceless for its other-worldliness when redeemed, perilous if left unmined and unrefined.

But when Mom approached her about suing Neil Diamond, she had neither practical advice nor commiseration to offer. I don't think she got past those words: "'Neil Diamond is harassing me in my head.'" She didn't question Mom's sanity, or hint that Mom might need psychiatric intervention. Mom was already in so deep that Grandma didn't even try to talk her out. All she said was that there was no way to support a case for psychic harassment; it was a lost cause, so she wouldn't help to initiate a lawsuit.

That was one of two fights I witnessed between them. I still hear Mom's hurt and disappointed voice as we left Grandma's house: "'I should have known better than to expect any help from *you*.'" Words that scorched the air like toxic old fumes, words that suggested long-ago hurts, terrible secrets from the past... "'I should have known better than to expect any help from *you*.'" What did *that* mean? The Grandma *I* knew was the dear woman who took in her daughter and four grandchildren, who nurtured and protected us when we were most in need. Could she ever have been anything but kind and generous? And how disquieting to hear those bitter words from my mother, who'd raised us to love and honor our grandparents as we loved and honored her. Could my soft-spoken, cheerful, always courteous mother ever have been otherwise?

(She *had* been otherwise: the other fight—we never talked about it because I could see it brought up a heartbreaking memory of remorse and shame. As a child in a fit of rage she slammed a door, and the dear kitten that followed her everywhere was in the wrong place at the wrong time. Its neck was broken and it died. Grandma mentioned it as an object lesson against temper tantrums to one of us, and Mom's hurt was evident—she felt betrayed by Grandma's revelation. I hope she found the immense power of forgiveness, finally.)

Too bad Grandma couldn't talk Mom into getting some professional help—but she couldn't. Crazy was either something you hid or something you painted with; it wasn't something you talked about. And since there was a big job to do, namely raising four kids, well she'd better just do it, and stop scaring people to death by talking like a madwoman.

At some point early in her obsession Mom was still able to recognize how far outside normal parameters her thoughts and feelings had progressed. In 1976 she went to see a psychologist in Toronto. She took me with her. He listened carefully, and carefully didn't say she was nuts. She'd have asked that question directly, too. She sincerely wanted to know that she *wasn't* nuts, but she never again sought advice from a mental health professional about her telepathic affair. The psychologist didn't say much else; he tried to set up another appointment, but Mom saw no need to go back. Even during the years she spent bouncing around the psychiatric wards of local hospitals in treatment for bi-polar disorder, she held on to her belief that Neil Diamond was her soul-mate. She revealed to me as recently as 1996, when she was nearly sixty, that she was "'still getting messages from California'". I was a dutiful daughter; I listened. But I wasn't a good, kind, compassionate daughter: I was a coward who didn't ask her to elaborate, and didn't try to set her straight, either.

I wish I'd done one or the other.

I've read about 'star-stalkers'—people who have my mother's illness, who are convinced that they are somehow attached to celebrities, that they have a right—even a moral obligation—to make public the ties that exist only in their heads. Mom was either too gracious or too proud to air her psychic partnership with Neil Diamond. Or perhaps she always knew, deep down, that no such relationship existed. Maybe the fear of acknowledging and facing her demons was bigger than her courage. (If this *isn't* a relationship with Neil Diamond, what is it?)

But for me it was long years suspended in a nebulous tension of neither belief nor unbelief. It must have been sometime in my late twenties that I finally allowed the thought to rise: "Her 'relationship' with Neil Diamond is an aspect of her illness." For many years I held with party policy—Neil Diamond caused Mom's nervous breakdown because he was enjoying the very best of both worlds. He was divinely attached to my mother, and would never leave her heart or head; and he would never walk away from the comfort of his life to take on the complications of hers.

'Above all, love each other deeply, because love covers over a multitude of sins.' 1 Peter 4:8

Restless October weather pulls every which way. It makes me want to stay home and bake pies, and it aggravates old wanderlust. Years ago on the yellow school bus the rural gravel roads were transformed on a dull and rain-whipped day. They took me to school, just like every other weekday from September to June, but the world outside the bus window was magically different. The muddy brown field beside the Bauer farmhouse, with its brush-lined creek, hid a secret. Though I never saw them, I just *knew* Gypsies must be camped in a spare, scrubby copse of stunted wild apple trees, swamp willows, and thorn plums. Their wagon would be settled invisible as a grouse among the trees, cozy and warm inside, ready to blow away with the right wind. Many times on the ride to school, my wandering daydream self sloshed cold and wet along a puddled, mucky trail through brisk March rain, or gusty smoke-smelling November drizzle. The Gypsy people would be waiting for me, chilly and red and cheerful.

They'd sit in a circle around a rain-spattered campfire and offer me something hot to drink, sassafras tea or cider... They were never surprised to see me. They were like Grandma: colour, warmth, laughter.

I wandered away a lot. Sometimes I daydream-wandered on winter nights, walking backwards through the snowy moonlit woods. Lou and the twins usually came along with me; and Napper of course. In my dream the twins would be bundled up, half-reclining on the toboggan, wrapped like wintering cocoons. We'd build a fire and be safe. Kid logic meant no-one would find us in the morning, because of course our footprints didn't lead away from the house, but back to it. It would be a big mystery. Sometimes I entertained a hazy notion of hitching a ride, alone, on a passing freight train, to someplace warm and far away. But mostly we just stayed in a safe circle together. Lou and I would take care of the twins. My childish self never imagined Mom and Dad's devastation; how tried, convicted, and disowned by the judgment of lost and merciless me. I didn't hate them—I loved them as any child loves its parents—but I didn't feel safe at home, and I was truly convinced I could do a better job raising us.

I still love to walk in the woods, a good gift my father gave me. Though I hiked many more miles with Mom, my earliest memories of Dad are woods memories. Three or four- year-old me, with young and sprightly Napper, in the woods with Dad; Dad settling little me comfortably in a protected nook at the base of a big maple, still safe and loved, while he went on ahead with his gun. There was no fear or loneliness, only "shhhhh", and waiting tucked against my tree, and walking. We walked out of the woods and back to the house through stubble or furrowed fields, me holding his hand, Napper loping ahead, ears a-flop, or trotting nose-down and tail up alongside. Dad hunted; sometimes there'd be game in his bag, sometimes just mushrooms. Sometimes I rode his shoulders home. Dad was a transplanted city boy, but it was he who taught me to move so quietly and deliberately in the woods that the animals forgot I was human.

My mother and father got married because they 'had to'; I was the result of my poor mother's first sexual experience. I don't think they'd known each other even a full year by the time I was born six months after their wedding. I did the math once, and discovered I was conceived right around Halloween of 1958. My mom was only nineteen, and my dad twenty-three. I have an idea of them at least half-drunk after a staff Halloween party—they both worked at the same factory—making out in my dad's brand new sky-blue TR3. They parked on Beechwood Road, a rural road on the butt-end of the Niagara Escarpment; and that's how I started cooking. This image doesn't embarrass me, I suppose because they were complete strangers to one another again by the time I heard about my earthly conception. So in my image they're just good-looking young folks from the 50s, looking for a little action. A movie image.

They *were* kids playing grown-up; a pair of bewildered youngsters married to each other and ready to give it the old college try. Lots of people made marriages work back then, with little else to go on. I've tried to look at my parents' liaison within the context of great social and cultural upheaval—it was the sixties after all—but no matter how hard I look, what I really see is a couple of lost souls. They didn't know or like each other very well, and neither of them was mature enough to recognize and work past their flaws.

Growing up, we didn't know our parents were merely human. We didn't know about the dark side of our mom's childhood: the screaming rage-filled tantrums that kept everyone at bay, so that

Grandma gave up trying to enforce discipline when it was Mom's turn at chores. We didn't know our dear mother was flawed, that she sometimes misperceived events, maybe even on purpose, to make herself the victim. We didn't know what made our father tick—what made him sometimes tick and tick and tick, and finally explode.

If they were still alive their grandchildren would see other truths. They'd have grown into their better, wiser, selves; affectionate old people who'd share memories of "when your mother was little..."

What terrible thing happened to my mother and father, that didn't happen to my grandmother and grandfather, or to my aunts and uncles? (*Was* it something that happened to them? Or did each of them bring a defect that, under the catalyst of circumstance, combined to destroy their partnership? Or were they just weak and defenceless, at the mercy of the big, bad world...?)

Somebody dropped the ball along the way, and now it has to be untangled, a giant, snarled string, leading back and back, showing us where we came from. Backwards footprints through the snowy woods...

CHAPTER 4

School started three months before the twins were born, and I became 'Bucky Beaver' soon after. That was the year my adult overbite grew in, huge, gapped front teeth that stayed too big for my skinny face 'til I was grown up. The teacher, bless her heart, started 'Bucky Beaver' in an affectionate attempt to discourage my pencil-eating habit. It didn't take long for the class to pick it up, minus the affection. Miss Alexander couldn't have known how that appellation would stick and warp me.

In those days, the fat, red-painted eraser-less pencils we used had to be returned at the end of every school day. Mine was always chewed to soggy shreds, and when an unfortunate classmate picked my pencil out of the box next day, its frayed end resembled a paintbrush, and it was still damp with saliva.

Mom was busy with babies George and Joanie, and she still had Lou home, too, the year I started school. At first she conscientiously got up with me every school day morning, made my breakfast, brushed out my hair and put it in neat braids or pigtails—and I was just like all the other little girls. But soon I was getting myself up and ready for school. It didn't bother me much if there were no clean clothes, or my socks didn't match. If Mom was in bed, she couldn't see me leave with hair in tangled knots, and she couldn't nag me to brush my teeth.

Starting in grade four or five I slept with a tongue depressor held against my jutting Bugs Bunny incisors by a big elastic band that went around the back of my head. I wanted braces the way other kids wanted ponies or bicycles, but I didn't see a dentist until I was eighteen years old and could pay for it myself. The tongue depressor worked, to a degree: the gapped overbite is still there, but it's no longer worthy of caricature. Yet I was well into my twenties before I allowed myself to smile the way God meant me to: a toothy, corny grin, more goofy than pretty, one that leaves others no choice but to smile back. Alfred E. Newman *is* cute, in his own puckish way.

In elementary school I learned to tell stories; I was a Martian, for instance, with a spaceship that took me home every night. It was just entertainment for me and whatever kid joined me at recess, but I liked the power of words and stories. My alien identity afforded me so much playground attention that I hung onto it well past its expiration date.

That, combined with my careless hygiene and fierce desire to do a gender swap, earned me a reputation as a weirdo early in my school career.

In 1966 boys had a lot more freedom and fun at school than girls did. Girls were still required to wear a dress or skirt, even when it was necessary to slog through thigh-high snow to catch the school bus. Pants were allowed underneath, but it was a get-up that hampered movement. So by grade two I'd made up my mind to become a boy. My 'plan' was transformation by determination: I intended to be male by age twelve through sheer force of will. I hated being a girl at school; at home it was perfectly natural for me to climb trees and wade in the creek, to catch grasshoppers and garter snakes. But at school those activities were strongly discouraged; the world seemed suddenly to favor boys.

We weren't poor until sometime after the twins were born: we had a large freezer down in the cellar, ("down cellar", we said) and a big vegetable garden, a car that ran (nobody had more than one car back then) and we went on family camping trips in summer.

Sometimes cars slowed down, and people admired our house as they drove past. Dad kept our large yard neatly mowed, and Mom had beautiful flower beds all over the property. I loved to stand in the midst of the great clumps of bronze and purple and yellow irises growing in the damp soil at the woodsy edge of our lot, to bury my face in the sweet July scent. In spring, I sat in a secret little space under the honeysuckle bush with Bib, our plush blue and white cat, and drank in tender April. Tall, gracious elms stood like benevolent giants along the road in front of our tidy little house. Napper used to snooze in a snug hollow at the base of one of their trunks, curved as though custom made for his curled-up body. Sometimes I'd nap with him, resting my head on his warm ribs. On chilly days, we'd face the sun, and I'd tuck my cold fingers under his floppy black ears.

When we were old enough, Lou and I played alone down by the creek in the woods behind our house. We called it 'the crick'; and that's what it was until Miss Wingman corrected me in grade two by informing me that in Canada, it was pronounced 'creek'.

That was 1967, Canada's centennial year, and in our little corner of the world, Dad wasn't the only adult around who hated Americans: the easiest way to demonstrate your patriotism was to be anti-American. Miss Wingman told me that Americans said 'crick'. "You don't want to sound like an American, do you?" I most certainly did not! I brought home 'creek' the way my cousin brought 'wash' into our grandparents' house after he started school. Until then, instead of doing laundry, they did the 'worsh' at Grandma's house, and the kids had to go and 'worsh up' for supper.

It was Miss Wingman who crushed my dream of growing up to marry Robert Louis Stevenson, until then as alive and dear to me as my own family. His poems captured my child heart so utterly that I just *knew* we'd marry as soon as I grew up. "No you won't," she said in her brisk voice, hard careless words that slammed a door. "He's been dead almost a hundred years." Icy, shocking words, they locked the door forever.

It was Miss Wingman who finally told me to 'sit down and shut up', as I wandered, humming a tune, out of my seat for the umpteenth time, and crossed the classroom to the big daydream window. My work was done, and I was bored. At home I was encouraged to go outside and play. Could walking over to look out the window really be such a terrible crime?

But it was also Miss Wingman who encouraged me as I wrote my first story. "Why do you want to know how to spell 'smithereens'?" she asked, but she good-naturedly spelled it out for me when I insisted that another, simpler word wouldn't do.

I didn't say 'crick' out loud again. But forever in my heart it remained 'the crick.'

The creek had a bridge, a crumbling old concrete structure that at one time likely accommodated tractors and hay wagons, but the road through the woods and across the creek had long since gone back to nature. There weren't even ruts left: only a wide treeless trail down a hill that always detoured to dump our toboggan a little closer to the creek than was comfortable, especially in late winter when the ice got punky. The creek was as unequivocally our territory as our own backyard. A hundred picnics were eaten there, cheese and apples and hardboiled eggs lovingly peeled, salted, and wrapped in tinfoil by Mom.

Lou and I were queens of the woods: master frog-and-snake-catchers, professional tree-climbers, artisan fort-builders, fearless explorers, competent foragers. We knew where to find every hickory tree, every wild apple and pear tree. We knew where to find touch-me-not growing, the plant that cures the crazy itch of poison ivy. We knew where they all grew: every patch of spring beauties, hepaticas, trilliums, and dog-tooth-violets. We knew you could eat purple violets, but not May apples.

In the woods across the road, there was our own version of Okefenokee Swamp, a knee-deep stretch of stinking black muck and brackish water loved by Napper. We knew of a maple tree whose canopy was so overgrown by wild grape vines that we could lie down on it, twenty-five feet above the earth, as confidently as we might lay on our living-room floor. There was our 'highway tree', a straight-trunked giant that had gone down in a windstorm, and leaned against its neighbor at a thirty degree angle. A brave kid could walk a very long way up the highway tree.

One year, late February, Lou and I tapped a small stand of swamp maples, rising early to make the trek into the still-snowy woods, slogging back to the house with heavy plastic pails full of pink sap. Mom boiled it down to syrup for us.

Early each September, in the fields bordering our woods, we knew it was time to watch out for the big black and yellow garden spiders that bided so elegantly in the orb webs they hung between goldenrods. Every ditch and pond, every creek and April puddle-full of frog eggs, every field of bursting milkweed pods and spiky teasel was ours.

I tell these things so my children will have an inheritance, so they'll know where else they came from, the other people that are theirs. They have to be gathered together, the people who are left, and the stories still untold.

Am I telling myself a true story, too? I thought I knew what happened: Mom and Dad got married too young, too many kids came too fast, Dad started drinking and carousing. Mom packed us up and left, and then broke from the strain of trying to raise four kids on next-to-nothing. My own life seemed destined to be a major screw-up, too—or worse, a mediocre one. Did I get here by looking for adventure or did I just chicken out and run away, leaving all the mess behind? What am I doing? Trying to go back and fix stuff I ran away from long ago? Am I only scrapbooking?

There was *something* further back than lost and frightened; there was a time *before*. There is a time after—and they who finally look back from safety must light the way for those following.

CHAPTER 5

I remember watching the Fleischer Brothers' cartoons on Saturday mornings on the black-and-white TV in Grandma and Grandpa's den. Before Sunday matinee Tarzan and afterschool Superman, before James Arness as Marshall Matt Dillon, and William Shatner as Captain James T. Kirk, there was Popeye the Sailor Man. Secretly, I believed my grandfather was the real Popeye. There was the same anchor tattooed on his forearm, and Grandpa was as strong and noble as Popeye, though considerably taller. When I was very young, he smoked a pipe like Popeye's. It didn't matter that blonde and shapely Grandma wasn't Olive Oyl—Grandpa was certainly my hero Popeye.

Grandpa built their house, and it was made of music and art, and full of objects long-loved and steeped in family lore. The windows were much bigger than those in our little rented country bungalow, and there were bookshelves built in beneath them. In the den was a fieldstone fireplace, with a tall chimney and wide hearth. The fireplace tools delighted us—kid-sized brass broom and dustpan, poker and tongs. A solid bronze spaniel with glass eyes lay on the hearth, loved by all the grandchildren. On the walls hung the kinds of pictures I had to look at, to dream into: a huge, ornately gilt-framed jigsaw-puzzle western scene—wild horses thundering across the plains, smoky mountains in the background. Pictures sketched and painted by Grandma and 'the girls', bowls and table legs lathed by Grandpa and 'the boys'... How we loved the shrunken head crafted by Grandma: a work of art that grimaced down at us with bright black hatpin eyes from the wall over the piano—an apple, face-carved, years-shrivelled, and wonderfully grisly, hung by a hank of her own greying hair.

※

November has blown in like a sloppy drunk. Incontinent—doesn't know whether to rain or shine, so it does both, sometimes at the same time. Seedy looking, too; brown and tattered, full of holes, messy. Doesn't matter how solicitously you try to clean it up—rake leaves, wipe muddy feet—November can't stay tidy. November the ranting prophet, seeing ahead to winter and death. A crazy old man who knows the end is near, whose hysterical laughter laments lost youth, grieves inevitable winter, and scorns those who cannot yet imagine a spring that dares bloom without them. November knows.

My mantel looks nice with a vase of luminous red and yellow maple leaves, but the hearth is tracked by cat footprints. His feet are always wet and muddy this time of year. He's usually a fastidious cat, but I guess like me, he gets tired of pointlessly cleaning up after November.

What's this? So it's November, and winter here gapes before us too much like an open grave. The cold, dark, and wet will have to be endured 'til April, when spring finally rises reluctantly out of the earth and sky. Back home in the east, spring *springs,* clearly a resurrection; here on the west coast it labours upward more like a weary zombie fighting its way out of a tight-fisted grave. When west-coast spring manages to stand up fully awake at last, it faces a herd of surprised and cautious crocuses. They've been up since

January, poor things; here the earth doesn't freeze, so the spring flowers get up early, and have to wait like threadbare children for the sun's frugal May warmth. But it is spring, so we welcome it; summer follows inevitably. Even when *that* spring comes—the one without me here to see it—it'll be welcome, because I'll be Home for that one.

When the kid I used to be heard the midnight freight train and dreamed of far away, she didn't know that the home you leave behind goes on without you. She didn't know about west-coast November, either—the cold, inexorable rain that washes steadily at the surface tension of every moment, blurs the present away, takes you back and back, behind mountains and prairies, all the way back to home far away.

But of course, home *has* gone on without you. So even though you can't really leave, you can't go back, either. You can only go Home, eventually, and do your best to make sure everybody else knows the way, too, so they'll all be there for the big reunion.

I hope I don't die in the wintertime. Lots of people do; they die right after New Year's, because they spend themselves on their resolve that death not spoil anybody's holidays. Thoughtful of them…

Mom died in the winter, just after her sixty-seventh birthday. Sometimes it still doesn't seem like she's gone. I find myself thinking, oh, I'll have to tell Mom about this or that funny thing one of the kids has said, and then there's that jolt—no, I can't share any of their triumphs or trials, she's not there to offer advice, or tell me a story of a similar trait she worried about in me. We can't even share recipes; I miss her telling me to use a 'glop' of butter. I'm sorry I can't tell her I finally know how much a glop is.

For a long time it bothered me that she died in winter; spring was her favorite season, and she looked forward to it each year with the enthusiasm of a kid. Her letters, like the long-distance phone calls we shared, were full of small, chatty news about her garden. When the crocuses and snowdrops poked their brave shoots through the Ontario snow, we knew that once again spring had triumphed. But Mom went on ahead to God's spring that year, and we didn't get to talk about it.

When I was 15, we'd drink coffee and discuss deep spiritual and philosophical matters until dawn; often I'd skip school the next day. No topic was out of bounds. What an honor it was for awkward young me to watch and listen while my fearless mother threw herself at the sky. How encouraging she was as I groped my own way toward consciousness.

But she went without a safety net; she went without any navigation aid except her own uninhibited and unbalanced imagination. I followed her until I couldn't, but by then it was too late: I was no longer able to be honest with her. Visiting her when she was dying was like the long-ago days that I dropped by her house after work. Back before I headed west, I'd often stop in just for a visit, or to bring her money for coffee and cigarettes. We'd sit and smoke and drink coffee, but though I'd listen to all she had to say, I kept the Neil Diamond stuff locked in a separate little room in my head. I could not say, "Mom, I can no longer fully believe that you have a psychic bond with Neil Diamond." It was easy to not talk about it: I no longer believed wholeheartedly, but neither was my unbelief complete. The failure to admit my ambivalence set a terrible precedent. Years later, relieved that she was going to church, and therefore involved in some kind of normal community, I did not ask the only question that mattered: "Mom, are you safe; are you ok with dying?"

I did not ask.

She was so weak, only a month away from death, when I went to see her. It was shocking. It had only been five years since I'd last seen her, but cancer had taken her past the point of no return. I could see the truth in her eyes: she knew she was dying. Why couldn't I allow myself to be weak, to break down and cry the way I wanted to? At least then we could have talked about it, we could have had some truth between us. Instead we stole an olden day, going for a long drive in the southern Ontario winter countryside, and I could see her eyes looking past and beyond.

Instead I read aloud to her, around the giant lump in my throat, from some stupid murder mystery she'd gotten from the hospital thrift shop. There was that ambiguous comment she made when I asked if she'd like me to get a book for her, "It had better be a short one," terrible comment, Mom, why? Because you know I'm only here for a week or because you aren't sure you'll make it to the end of the story? Or was that an opening for me, one that I was too cowardly to jump into? It sounded like one of the wry observations that were so typical of her comic take on life's bleak moments; was it meant to assure me that her sense of humour was still intact? Or did she mean to say "Talk to me about reality,"?

God forgive me, I did not ask.

It's time to start the Christmas baking. My friend's youngster, a mostly merry fellow of five, is more interested in watching cartoons than 'helping'. It's good to have a friend for a neighbor—our relationship reminds me of country neighborliness, where you know that if your kid isn't home from school, he's at their house. He'll get fed if he hangs around long enough, and she'll send him home once he's outstayed his welcome. She hasn't got any illusions about him, because she's seen him grow; likewise, she won't be mortally offended if I speak firmly to her child. It's a friendship that deserves particular honor because it relies on old-fashioned graciousness. My friend didn't know me back when I lived the facade; she has seen the honest worst of me from the beginning of our relationship. She's seen my house when the boys' bedroom floor was ankle-deep in clothes and toys, she's experienced dinner cancellations because I'm cranky and unsociable, and she's taken my youngest child at a moment's notice. She has given me gifts of wonderful practicality and love. Her generosity has been so easy and unselfconscious that when I look around my house and catalogue all the blessings that have come from hers, I'm astonished. Yet this is the daily, ordinary—extraordinary—friendship of a neighbor. "'Lord, who is my neighbor?'" I take it for granted, and I hope she does, too.

CHAPTER 6

It seems to be wintertime a lot in my earliest memories. I particularly recall how every Christmas, Dad warned us, "It's going to be mighty lean this year, kids; don't expect too much from old Santy Claus." Or "Don't get your hopes up; we're in for a grim Christmas." But we knew better: "We don't care!" we piped up. We *didn't* care; we knew Christmas would come with the same magic it brought every year, and that no matter how many or few the gifts under our tree, our hearts and bellies would be filled to bursting. Most years, we'd join the rest of the family at Grandma and Grandpa's or an aunt and uncle's house Christmas Eve, and there'd be food and laughter and music.

Later, on the drive home, we'd listen to the car radio for the CBC updates on Santa's progress, anxious to make it home and into bed before he landed at our house. One year, I was sure I saw the lights of his magic sleigh in the inky sky over the woods near our house. And one Christmas time, I peered hard into the winter night as we drove by neighbors' houses, few and far between along our dark and snowy country road. As always, I was trying to see into those warm places, to feel the cosy family times that I knew must be going on behind those mellow lighted windows. We were alone, Dad and I, or maybe the other kids were asleep; we sang Christmas carols, and got to wondering about angels. Dad asked how many angels I thought could fit on the head of a pin, and then explained that since angels were beings of spirit, they operated under a different set of laws. Wonder and curiosity thrilled together in me, recognizing *something*, and both the conversation, and the sense of having shared a special time with Dad, stayed with me forever.

There was never a grim Christmas: not even one. Now, of course, I know he was just trying to protect his children from disappointment. But back then, I only wanted our dad not to let those bleak, hard little words out of his mouth: "grim Christmas," "lean Christmas."

Animals were a big part of our family; Napper was a constant companion, joining our rambles through the woods and fields like a protective older brother. We always had a cat, sometimes two, once fourteen. That happened before I started school, when two lady cats had litters within days of one another. An old black-and-white photo shows my young and handsome father, an animal lover, feeding new kittens with an eyedropper. One of the mother cats had disappeared; her sister wasn't able to manage all thirteen kittens, so Mom and Dad took turns nursing them from an eyedropper and a doll's bottle. 'Old Ma' was what we called that mama cat; two of the kittens, Tiger and Blackie, needed rescuing from our cistern later that summer after they fell in while Dad had the lid off for cleaning.

Bib was Napper's feline brother for many years; he was a large, easy-going cat who didn't seem to mind Lou and me tucking him into our doll cradle and rocking him to sleep. Pragmatic, as cats are, he simply purred and snoozed. When I was six, Bib's death broke all of our hearts. He often trekked up to Arlen Keller's milk barn to get another breakfast along with the Keller barn cats. One day he came home dragging his hind legs. Mom and Dad figured he'd been kicked or stepped on by one of Arlen's Holsteins; we didn't think he'd been hit by a car, because Bib didn't go on the road. It was faster to go across the field, and there was the added bonus of a possible mouse. Mom rigged up a little sling for him, but poor Bib's back was broken, and though he gamely dragged himself around for a couple of days, it was clear he wouldn't get better. He was Mom's cat; they took him to the vet and had him put to sleep. Mom cried when they told us, and together we buried him in the back yard.

When I was only three or four, Dad and Arlen found a red-tailed hawk chick out of the nest, and brought it to our house. Dad built a cage for Pacheeper—that's what Dad named him—on top of the doghouse that Napper never used. Sometimes young Pacheeper rode on Napper's back. Napper wasn't just a good-natured dog—he was heroic around any young creature, animal or human. Once when the whole family was outside enjoying a sunny day in the yard, George and Joanie got into some sort of mischief. Dad grabbed a twin to apply a swift spank, and Napper was on him like a fury. His jaws clamped Dad's wrist, and he growled, low and serious. He didn't bite - there was no broken skin: but he didn't let go, either. No terrible blow-up followed Napper's apparent betrayal—Dad didn't curse either his child or his dog. I think he was secretly proud of Napper's noble intervention.

Dad taught Pacheeper to fly by tossing him into the air. After he matured and flew away for good, Dad would sometimes take a handful of raw ground beef into the field across the road from our house, and stand with an outstretched arm while calling his hawk. And Pacheeper would appear, at first just a dot circling high in the sky. Down and down he spiralled, getting bigger with every turn. Eventually he landed on Dad's arm, and Dad rewarded him with the raw meat.

There was a squirrel, too, towards the end of my parents' marriage; Petey was another orphan baby, a foundling from my Grandma Adamson's back yard. Grandma Adamson couldn't look after a young squirrel, and her dear old cat Tommy, a sleek and complacent butterfly tabby, certainly wouldn't have tolerated Petey's caffeinated personality. Petey didn't last long. A squirrel is a high-octane kind of animal, not really a creature you can cuddle. Pete was best at scrambling up your leg inside your jeans, just as if you were an odd smooth-barked species of tree, using his sharp little claws all the way. When Petey disappeared into the woods, we were all a bit relieved, especially the cat. Nobody looked for him.

And there was the time Lou and I brought a very special brood of mice into the house.

We sometimes skated on a large windswept puddle in the field across the road; it was closer than the creek, though you had to manoeuvre around the occasional wheat stalk sticking up through the bumpy ice. We sat on snow-covered humps, left after Arlen had done his fall furrowing, to change into our skates. One year, perhaps we were nine and seven, Lou and I kicked the snowy top off a hump, hoping to find rodent tunnels, and found instead a nest of several baby field mice, still hairless, frozen into a solid ball. Full of pity for those tiny lives, lost before they'd even begun, we hoped they might revive once we warmed them up, an early experiment in cryogenics.

We took them home, nestled them gently into a cloth-lined shoebox, covered them with a doll blanket, and stuck the shoebox in the bottom drawer of a dresser. Once they thawed, Lou and

I petted the soft little bodies, talked to them, and sang tender lullabies. Our baby mice didn't wake up, but they did begin to emit a peculiar odour. I was impressed by the acuity of Mom's nose the day she stood, puzzled and sniffing, in our bedroom doorway. "Why does it smell like dead mice in here?" she asked.

I remember going to the senior Keller's farm kitchen on winter mornings; like Bib, I often got a second breakfast before Grandpa Keller or one of the boys drove Liza and I up to the corner to catch the bus. Liza was in high school, but she let me sit beside her on the bus; Big Knees and Little Knees, my six-year-old self called us. Grandma Keller would hail me in every snowy cold morning, and I'd somehow have time to unwrap and sit at her table amongst her three or four strapping sons, and daughter Liza, and eat.

Her breakfast table was an old-fashioned mid-chores farm feast: good hot food, and plenty of it. If Mom was up early I'd already have been fully fortified by oatmeal or cream-of-wheat, slathered with butter and brown sugar—but I'd still manage at least an egg or a couple of pieces of bacon and toast at the Keller table. Grandma Keller was always trying to fatten me up; I was taken aback to see cake at the breakfast table, and outright scandalized when she offered me butter for it. At my house, cake was a birthday dessert, and it came with icing. You didn't eat cake for breakfast, and it certainly didn't get buttered.

The old Keller farmhouse was a reliable comfort to me, especially after Arlen and Elsa sold their place next door to us—next door was still a full third of a mile away—and moved a few miles up the road. Arlen was the eldest of the Keller boys; before they moved, his two sons were Lou's and my closest playmates. At just three, I remember standing on the foot bar of the old-fashioned baby carriage while Mom wheeled Lou up the road to sit sharing tea and gossip with Elsa, who was then as comfortable to me as my own dear mom. I loved tall Arlen, too, with his deep, gentle voice. Those days long ago I sat and played under the Keller kitchen table with Ben, while babies Lou and Davie napped together. When we were a few years older, I rode with Ben in the wagon behind his dad's combine, stood laughing with him under a dusty shower of oats or wheat, caught innumerable stink bugs.

Sometimes the two of us perched on the running boards of Arlen's big red Massey Ferguson tractor while he ploughed or baled hay. Ben and I were inseparable for the first six years of my life, as close as brother and sister; but because his birthday was on the other side of December, I started school a year sooner. Ben was so mad at me for going off to school without him that he followed me all the way home from the bus stop corner one day, hurling dirt clods. When they moved, Lou and I were alone; Grandma Keller was Ben's grandmother, but she saw how lost I was without him, and treated me like one of her own.

I loved the old Keller farmhouse, but mostly Grandma Keller's kitchen, which, though clean, seemed always messy. Now that I have children I understand why her cupboard doors were never shut, and why there was always a warm good-food smell wafting through the air.

So what is it about that magic word, *home*...? 'In my Father's house are many mansions...'

House, home, mansion; I keep looking for it, and I keep getting glimpses—just enough to keep me seeking. On a drive or walk I see it, or maybe in a dream—always around a curve or over a rise... Sometimes in a rush of recognition tied only to the smell of melting snow and apple blossoms, or a few poignant bars of half-heard music. I don't know why it's in me to yearn, or why it was given to me to have an image upon which to hang the longing.

But I *can* see it. Knowing home is like the moment you become aware—finally—that you aren't really alone; that the Presence has been—is—with you all along. You'd think after *that* revelation there wouldn't be room for longing; there wouldn't be a need for something as prosaic as 'home'. But if I believe the Presence is with me, that He has plans for me, then I must also believe He put the longing in me, and that as long as I continue with 'ask, seek, knock', I'll get there.

There are days, though, that seem hopelessly far from home. January days, February days; days it almost seems best just to lie down and go to sleep in a snow bank, if only one was available.

There were plenty of snow banks around when I was a kid—that was when everything was bigger, days were lighter and longer, and we didn't care what time it was, or that there were only twenty minutes between now and the next necessary task. A snow bank was a manageable mountain: something to scramble up and slide down. One winter, maybe 1966, Dad dug out a little house for Lou and me, our own snug bear cave hollowed out of an eight foot cliff of shovel-piled snow in our country driveway.

Sometimes on winter nights we were miners: diamonds lay as casually around our yard as hastily-brushed toast crumbs—shocking display of riches, but we were vulgar poor kids, so we loved it. Even better than going after moonlit snow diamonds were the nights we were sugar miners, triumphantly possessive of the Demerara deposits found only alongside the driveway.

Cars ran on cheap dirty gas then, and engines warmed up for fifteen minutes or more those deep, quiet, bitterly cold Ontario winter mornings. Rural evenings, with no streetlight but the moon, the snow beside the driveway turned into lovely glittering brown sugar.

CHAPTER 7

One thing I know is that my Father's house won't have any scary secret rooms; like the farmhouse we moved into after Mom and Dad split up, it'll be full of light and air, high ceilinged and many windowed. (What about those dream houses? There's that secret night-time place, just a cellar hole with sky for a roof, and for furniture, an old rusty chrome-and-vinyl kitchen chair, broken and abandoned. It's frightening, because it's clearly waiting for a condemned person—me—and no grace, no mercy, in sight. And the dream farmhouse: it looks and feels like home-at-last, yes, until you come all of a sudden to that upstairs room—the playroom—and there's a hole in the floor, or you try to go down the formal front stairs and find that a whole wing of the beautiful old place leans precariously, ready to break off into...what? Oblivion. You find it's much safer to fly than to walk. But even flying is perilous: the air is mote-filled and ghosty, as dusty and narcotic as the air in a hayloft on an August afternoon. You wake up disquieted, not quite terrified, knowing something's not right, because while you're dreaming it feels enough like home that you could *almost* stay there forever, fooled. But you aren't really sure who else lives there, and there isn't any safe place to rest.)

When will home be a place of rest?

The dream houses are all starting to overlap: the house of secrets has shown up on the same property as the house of air and light. Things that have been locked a long time in lonely cellars are coming out into the light and revealing themselves. They aren't scary in the light: just sad.

Like the time I came out of my room to say goodnight to Dad: Mom was at work—she worked part-time weeknights at Zeller's when I was in seventh grade. Dad had weird friends by then, partiers who'd drink and laugh and play cards around our kitchen table. They were at least a decade younger than him; it seemed he and his new friends were trying to get different kinds of cool from each other. One was only about eighteen. He drove a new GTO, and both Mom and Dad mistakenly believed I had a preteen crush on him, or on his car. Washing his car was supposed to have been an honor unto itself. The truth was that he may as well have been eighty-one, as far as I was concerned; and I couldn't have cared less about his car. He gave me an Evening in Paris perfume gift set for Christmas that year, and I knew that Mom and Dad had put him up to it. I was embarrassed by their astonishing lack of insight. Did they see me at all, or only what they imagined a girl my age ought to be? Or did they hope I might become that girl, one day?

Dad had two other new friends that last year of their marriage, both of whom were flamboyantly gay. One night when Mom was at work, I came out to say goodnight to Dad, and stepped around the corner to find him sitting on our living room chesterfield locked in a passionate eyes-closed embrace with his friend. I scurried back to my bedroom as quickly and quietly as I could, puzzled and a bit shocked. To me, 'faggot' was just another catch-all schoolyard epithet, devoid of sexual connotation, a word applied to me as regularly as 'Fleabag' and 'Bucky Beaver'. I didn't know anything at all about homosexuality, but I trusted my reaction: I knew I wasn't supposed to have seen Dad and Marley like that.

It was another thing to worry about, but I stuffed it into the back of my mind, and didn't lose much sleep. There was always a more immediate worry—another school day to face, a morning of scrambling to find clean or matching socks, to find underwear that stayed up, or, failing that, a safety pin. Another day to practice endurance. No time to worry about the universe inhabited by my parents.

The places of peace and beauty were there back in those dirty days, in my head, or on the other side of the school bus window, and I went to them often.

Once, a long age ago, a story of great peace and beauty whispered in fully told. It feels like the memory of a dream, but I don't recollect having dreamed it. Maybe it's always been there...

A story teller visits. He's a man, neither young nor old. There's nothing outwardly remarkable about him. But the stories he tells are gifts—they are riches beyond compare, they are like rare and precious jewels, like music that sings universes into being. I can taste the words he spoke—they got into *my* mouth somehow, and here they are still, alive and round with substance. Magic words: I tell them and tell them, yet they do not diminish. He visited me and some other children. He brought us gifts. Before he left he said, "Listen for me, I'll call you again someday." When he tried to go we chased after him, laughing. If he was leaving, we were coming along.

The day was hot and sunny; we followed him over hills, along dusty footpaths, through swishing timothy and ripening oats. He turned many times and told us, smiling and laughing, that we must go back—that we couldn't come along yet, our parents wouldn't understand. But we persisted, so finally he stopped, and we sat down with him on golden sunburnt grass under the crooked skeleton of an apple tree, bare and gnarled and many years dead.

He sang and said, sang and said. We *knew* he loved us, and oh! how we loved him, too.

We sat in a circle around him: he called one little girl 'Princess'. Maybe it was me.

After a while he got up to leave, and again, loving him too much to stay behind, we followed. Then he said "Look! There's a surprise for you!" And he pointed back toward the apple tree.

Which, miracle, was no longer dead: still ancient and gnarled, but the old crippled branches could not be seen for leaves, for blossoms beyond abundance. Spring *sprang* from it in a triumphant halo of humming bees and perfume.

We ran back, joyful, surprised: we marvelled and laughed and remarked to one another. By the time we remembered to look back down the road, he was gone.

How can a thing like that be with you forever, you don't recall a time it wasn't there? I think the Storyteller was Him – the Familiar Stranger. And He *did* call my name again.

"'For I know the plans I have for you,' declares the Lord, 'plans to prosper you, not to harm you, plans to give you a hope and a future.'" Jeremiah 29:11

Another promise; I've made promises to my children based on promises made to me by my Father. Those long ago mornings were full of promise, especially summer mornings, waking up with that sense of anticipation, that certainty of my God-given place in the universe. Even during elementary school, fully aware of my pariah status by grade three, there was the sure knowledge that I was born to have adventure. I was...special. To whom, and for what reason, it never occurred to me to wonder.

A gift, those golden minutes before full anxious wakefulness—the feeling that something GREAT might happen, that the question mark which hung over the day represented not a threat, but a robust and rosy promise.

Sometimes, looking back, it's easy to see the rocks in the road, or the something shiny that shouldn't have been a distraction, but was. Other times the path seems to have narrowly missed a deadly pitfall. And always, more faithful than stars, there were signs pointing the way back.

Like Mrs. Hawthorne, my grade four teacher, whose kindness endeared her to me forever—when my leaf project was stolen by a classmate, who worked hard to write his name over mine convincingly, she awarded my work the 'C' it deserved, and then spoke about forgiveness. I wanted to hold tight to my outrage—usually it was my own integrity lacking, so it felt good to be the victim of another's dishonesty. But Mrs. Hawthorne was not willing to leave either David or me in the mess. She had David apologize to me, and she had me say out loud that I forgave him. And something happened: though I may have only obediently parroted the words, my resentment evaporated. Mrs. Hawthorne was in touch with God; our classroom was a peaceful place. When during music class she asked us what we'd like to sing, we happily chose the hymns she taught us, 'All Things Bright and Beautiful' and 'I Come to the Garden Alone'.

The same year, just outside the classroom window one fine May day, a classmate dared me to say the 'f-word', and I complied, loudly, because I'd have done anything then to seem cool. After recess, dear Mrs. Hawthorne spent half an hour talking to us about the importance of not giving in to peer pressure, of holding on instead to what we knew to be right. I knew then that she'd heard my expletive, but there was nothing in her manner to accuse me. Though Mrs. Hawthorne was nearing retirement by the time she taught my class, it was clear that she loved her calling. I wonder how many lives were influenced by her kindness and mercy.

And there was my bedroom door, cheaply panelled with dark-stained veneer. There was a thin man-shape limned by the grain, evocative of the Renaissance paintings I pored over in our encyclopedia—so like many depictions of Jesus I'd seen. Though I didn't pray beyond a rote recital of the Lord's Prayer before bed, the outline of Jesus on my door made me feel safe. Signs. He was always there.

"If only, if only..." I have excused myself: if only my father hadn't been an alcoholic who bullied his family and abandoned his children to poverty. If only my mother hadn't sacrificed her sanity on the altar of her imagination. If only they had known enough to teach us our true worth.

But how could they? They didn't know their own value—how could they possibly have known ours?

They tripped so blithely, so blindly, down fateful ways to wrack and ruin, dancing always to their own drummers. How many signs went unheeded, how many times was the still small voice drowned out by the clamour of the desperate, ravenous self? Mom was an artist; Dad was cool. He wanted to be a modern day country squire—our home was to be a place of camaraderie, laughter, and goodwill. Company was supposed to sparkle. And when company alone didn't sparkle, booze and drugs and innuendo glowed ruddy and hectic.

How wonderful and tragic they were in their egotistical flakiness. But they only wanted what I want, what everybody wants: security and significance—a safe haven to call home and a meaningful part in the great plan. How lost they were in those days; what a careening, terrifying ride we took together. Sadly, not one of us knew enough to hold on—not to God, not even to each other. The ride crashed, and we scattered, foolish in wounded shock, amnesiac strangers. We let each other wander away lost.

CHAPTER 8

When I was a kid, there was never any practical talk. No talk of going to university, no family vision—no "We'll stay home and camp in the back yard this summer, kids, because we're saving up to buy a house." Those were the final days of assuming that girls would grow up to be wives: my sisters and I would marry. Which we did; a lot more often than anybody hoped.

By the time I was eleven, I had a job mucking out kennels—a neighbor down the road raised Malamutes and Great Danes. I earned five dollars every week, of which I'd spend half on payday candy. Saturday after work I'd head up the road to the nameless little country store, and buy four or five chocolate bars, the only candy worthy of my consideration. Then home the back way with my chocolate treasures, Oh Henry, Sweet Marie, chewy, gooey Big Turk, and always Coffee Crisp: across a field behind the store, over the train tracks, through the woods and into another field, where I sat invisible upon a hollow log beside a forgotten cow pond. Surrounded by teasel and goldenrod, I ate all of the chocolate and hid the wrappers in the log.

I didn't share the candy, and I didn't save any of my pay; the balance of my earnings usually went for cigarettes for Mom and Dad. They had credit at the store; sometimes when they sent me for cigarettes, Mrs. Merrick packed me back home empty-handed because their bill had gotten too big. But she was never unkind to me, nor did she try to confiscate my weekly earnings.

Behind the store was a tiny grass strip country airport, home to a sky-diving club. By the time I was five I wanted to fly more than anything else in the world. What kid doesn't?

But here I am, an adult: it's late winter, and soon there'll be spring work to do—seeds to plant, weeds to pull: my kids are sprouts and saplings, and gardens take a lot of looking ahead, a lot of planning. Will this be the spring of revival, the spring of having enough faith to look back and see the tree miraculously alive?

How foolish, perhaps, to expect my mood to dovetail with the season. Never have I been more impatient of winter, nor longed so for sunshine and warmth. Age should be a time of lying companionably in the puddle of sunshine we've earned, both the companionship and the sun a balm for old brains and bones. But here I am barely into middle age, companionless, and with body already aching, bones complaining... I wonder to myself, how did I get to be this person? I look at my picture, taken just a summer ago, white-water rafting down a crazy wilderness river—a young woman's adventure. It felt like Heaven—like fearless freedom, playing in God's backyard.

But the face in the picture isn't a young, soft face; there are lines of disappointment, determination. The hair is white where it escapes from under the helmet, and the arms wielding the paddle are stringy. Behind the gleam of momentary joy in the eyes is the ancient thousand-yard stare of the chronicler: looking behind, looking ahead, watching and watching and always watching... Dispassionate regard runs on automatic, but interpreting, chronicling, learning from the past and planning for the future—that takes time. She records all, and then spends the dreaming present sewing the past to the future. Is memory time travel? I'm looking around here—back then—and finding stuff I missed in my hurry to get away the first time. Some is still junk, still sad; but some is gold. What happens when, wandering in olden days, you find treasure and bring it back? Has the past been changed, then?

Might the future be changed?

Somewhere around here is the skinny kid that used to be: she only looked a little way back, and kidlike, never really looked ahead. So for her, whatever was, was. I wish I could warn her, tell her to *listen* when He speaks to her.

Raising kids takes a lot of time and a lot of work, but along with the obvious rewards come some secret joys, like flying high on the swings at the local playground. Try doing *that* without kids, when you're a middle-aged adult. Even if you're a woman, you'll get sidelong looks. So today I went to a parade with my kids; I attended a parade. (What exactly *does* one do at a parade?) There were marching bands, Shriner clowns, little girls with batons and shiny skirts, old-fashioned fire engines, war veterans. I watched them pass, cheered them on, nodded in time, and waved at them; there went friends and neighbors, even though I didn't know a single one by name.

There's something about a parade: something about people singing and dancing in the streets—we recognize it. A foreshadow, maybe, of the day we're all singing and dancing together in joyful triumph. Some like me cannot help but weep at the sound of bagpipes calling and calling, so wild and sweet even on a paved and line-painted North American city street. It's because we know the music of inexorable victory, of promises kept, faith justified. In our hearts we're all dance-marching along.

Grandpa's music called. I couldn't stay away from him when he disappeared into the den after supper; sometimes I planned to stay and play with my siblings and cousins, so I tried to ignore the chirps and zings that meant he was tuning up the fiddle. But he never got more than a few bars into "Turkey in the Straw", one of his warm-up pieces, before I was in there, sitting across from him, tumbled away in the music and watching, fascinated, while his old-man fingers nimbled over the strings. Grandpa was my pied-piper: the times I managed to stay out of the den for five minutes after he started playing, he'd look up with a twinkle in his eye and a grin on his face when I eventually showed up. "I wondered when you'd get here," he'd say. Some have to play, and some have to listen.

There were nights when all the good uncles, aunts, and cousins came over, too, and guitars krangled and jangled with the merry fiddle; Grandma might play two big soup spoons, wonderful rough-shod rhythm galloping clickety-clack alongside the strings. Once in a while somebody banged out chords on the piano, too. The grown-ups laughed and sang, and we all listened big-eyed, big-eared, our kid hearts stretched full to bursting because so much love and fun was swirled in with the smog of music and cigarette smoke.

Between songs came stories: "Remember the time you kids got so scared out on the lake, when you heard the bobcat scream? Oh, it was just like a banshee..." The stories were told over and over again, or maybe I've just remembered them over and over.

Grandma and Grandpa's house gave me the family times I want my children to know.

If there was a Google Time, I'd use it to get the bigger picture—look back over my past from a point somewhere nearer God... Someday I want to see how it all fits together—where the apparent chaos of every small, blind lifetime becomes a dancing pixilation essential to the biggest picture of all.

I want to see every person's part revealed, every act of evil redeemed. Of course it would be personal at first—I'd look for the meaning in Mom's illness and Napper's death. I'd want to see how He made my shallowness and infidelity work for the good of those who loved Him, how He used my subtle cruelties—those that were so carefully, so craftily, committed that I could almost deceive myself they had no root in ugly unkindness. What did He do with avarice posing as honest ambition, or vanity disguised as altruism? What about the grubby little transgressions that tarnish every human life, all those times we do what we don't want to do, in spite of knowing better, sometimes even in spite of His presence?

If there was a Google Time, I'd look for the crossroads of free will on the map of a lunatic's life, and ashamed of myself for needing to, I'd look to make sure there'd been signs left for him, too. Some of my brothers are madmen.

Heaven might have something like that: you get to see everything—first, the way it was originally intended, then a panorama of what actually occurred, and finally, with the details of redemption fully revealed.

You get to meet all those people—every human being there since the dawn of creation; you have eternity to get to know them, so no pressure. No cramming—it's not a vacation, you live here; you can go over to Grandma and Grandpa's house, maybe, for Sunday dinner. There's a good chance Jesus will be there—sure He's the King, but He's also everyone's brother. You can spend close, comfortable time with Mom again, without the need of any protection between you and delusion. They'll be the people He intended them to be from the beginning—Mom the artist, the warm, open person who just had to create, because she so loved the Father, and her best way of showing that was to imitate what He did. Dad, perhaps, as gracious nobleman—you can find out, finally, how to be your earthly father's daughter, take all the time you need. You can take a lifetime getting to know the nieces and nephews who grew up while you were far away licking old wounds, trying to see through a glass darkly. There will be all the time you need to follow every inchoate longing around every bend in the road, time to explore every high place in every mountain...

What a surprise for wanderlust—because that's when all those longings will be answered with, answered by, and answered for—JOY!

CHAPTER 9

'If you, then, though you are evil, know how to give good gifts to your children, how much more will your Father who is in Heaven give good gifts to those who ask...' Matthew 7:11

When I was a kid, I loved presents. On my seventh birthday, Grandma the poet gave me a Little Golden Book edition of Robert Louis Stevenson's *A Child's Garden of Verses*. I remember and love those poems still; the simple line and watercolor illustrations—black-masked robbers on a midnight garden wall—almost as captivating as the verses.

The same birthday, Mom and Dad got me a bicycle and my country-girl freedom increased exponentially. Grandpa accessorized it with a basket, horn, generator and lights. My bike was the best equipped in the countryside. The old-fashioned saddle was comfortable enough to ride for hours, and in those days if you wanted to take a side trip into the woods, or rest in the graveyard, you could safely leave your bike lying in the ditch. Everybody for miles around knew whose bike was whose, and nobody worried about theft.

Barbie was another gift; at Marsh Road School, all the girls—except me—played with their Barbie dolls at lunchtime and recess. Marsh Road School was an anachronism, a two-room brick schoolhouse left over from the turn of the last century, re-commissioned to accommodate the overflow from modern, bursting-at-the-seams Cook's Mills Elementary a couple of miles up the road. In 1968 Marsh Road School took a grade four class, and my grade three class.

Marsh was blessed with a pond at the edge of its wide yard; I spent most recesses mucking after frogs with the boys. Many days I came home with my pigtails undone and my socks muddy; after l getting into trouble a few times, I took off my socks and shoes, and went into the pond barefoot. Recesses with the boys at the frog pond were so much messy good fun that they were soon banned.

But the girls would have nothing to do with frog-catching, Barbie-less me. So I asked for a Barbie for Christmas that year, and got one from Grandma Adamson.

Dad called her 'Mother' and to us he referred to her as 'Nana'. 'Nana' was the name she called herself. But I couldn't say Nana: it was too delicate a name for my loud and buck-toothed country-girl mouth. You can hug a Grandma; you can climb onto a Grandma's lap. Even a Granny can be hugged, if you don't do it too hard. But a Nana might break, like the fancy china ladies who lived in perpetual curtsey on the end tables in her living room. Her lovely big house was full of beautiful furniture and carpets; you'd never find a marble or a Hot Wheels car on the floor, or see an unmade bed. There were no sun-melted crayons stuck to her windowsills, and you certainly couldn't write your initials in the dust on her dresser.

Her hair was always perfectly coiffed, but never in curlers, and her voice had a delicate, tinkling quality that I thought of as "silvery". In my mind she was Grandma Adamson; I can't recall using any affectionate title aloud to address her. Somehow it was formal, and even though I shared her last name along with her blood, there was something so regal and distant about her that I always left her home painfully aware of my peasant-like scabby knees.

Once, when I was fourteen and we'd already been away from Dad for a year, Mom took us to visit her. We lived at the farmhouse by then, and I was my new, free self, ranging blithely and fearlessly through fresh fields and streams. I bragged to my city grandmother about fishing in our new territory. I told her about wading in a slow, murky stream, about sitting on a log dam, rolling my jeans up and letting the cool, muddy water swirl around my hot legs and feet. With some relish at her discomfort, I described the shiny, mottled dark-brown leeches I found fattening up on my calves and ankles, how stubbornly they stuck and stretched when I tried to pull them off, and what a long time it took for the blood to finally stop its sluggish seep down my legs. "When are you going to start acting like a young lady?" she wanted to know; it seemed she'd been asking me that question forever, especially since the Barbie incident. I'd never measure up to my two cousins who lived there with her, tall, sure girls who got music lessons, whose bedrooms were feminine and frilly and never messy, who couldn't climb trees and probably didn't want to anyway. At fourteen, I didn't care for her opinion any more, and my fields and creeks were more important to me than my stiff and stilted relationship with Grandma Adamson.

But as a child I was intimidated by her.

On the rare Sunday we stayed at her house long enough for dinner—and it *was* dinner: we ate supper everywhere else—the food seemed always mysteriously ready. I never saw her cook, wash dishes, shop for groceries, or do any of the everyday chores that Mom and my other grandmother did.

How fitting that Barbie was a gift from Grandma Adamson; cold plastic Barbie made for a self-conscious, ritualized play that was rare for Lou and me. When I played with Barbie, I felt like an actress in a television toy commercial, acting the part of a kid for an invisible Barbie-buying audience.

Though I didn't love Barbie, I admired her hard Amazon figure with the fierce and hopeless envy of a kid who knew already that she was a misfit. I wanted Barbie because Barbie would be my ticket in: with Barbie in tow, I'd spend recess hanging out under the wooden steps of Marsh Road School with the other girls. At last I'd be part of that giggling, whispering, Barbie-owning entity. I couldn't wait for Christmas break to be over that year, so that I could bring her to school.

My absolute conviction left no room for doubt—Barbie would usher me triumphantly into that magic circle. So when my parents forbade me to take her out of the house, I was crushed. More than forty years later, though the pain and grief of The Barbie Incident has long since mellowed to soft and gently sad old memory, their decision still seems unfair and arbitrary.

How could I tell my shame to Mom and Dad? How could I explain that nobody liked their girl; that she was so awkward and strange that she had not a single friend among the girls at school? When I tried to tell about 'Bucky Beaver' and 'Fleabag': "They're only teasing you," said Mom and Dad, "just laugh, they'll stop." But they didn't, and ignoring the ugly names didn't help the situation, either, it just cemented me firmly into place as an outcast. After a while, you know Mom and Dad can't help it: they live in a different world, they don't *hear*. You stop trying to get them to listen, because even though at school you are so far past shame that pretty much anything could happen to you and it wouldn't touch you, at home it still matters what they say and think of you. And a stock response is no better than silence.

So when I was the only girl not invited to Jilly Houghton's birthday party that year, I lied to them that I'd lost my invitation, and went anyway, because I was hurt, because I didn't want Mom and Dad to find out that I really *was* just ugly old Fleabag. Fear turned my stomach as I got out of the car and walked alone up the gravel driveway to Jilly's front door. (What if they don't let me in? Where will I hide until Mom and Dad come back? I look back at the car—there's still time to turn around and admit the truth, but then I spy Jilly's leaning mailbox next to a deep ditch full of tall Queen Anne's lace, right in front of Jilly's house: I can crouch down in the ditch...) Then I'm at the door, and "*She's* not invited!" from Jilly amid a cluster of girls in the background, but Jilly's mother, warmly, "Certainly she is!" welcoming me in and hastily setting another place at the table. The colouring book I got wasn't new and clean, but half-scribbled throughout in purple crayon by Jilly's little sister, because, of course, I *hadn't* been invited.

Barbie would help me to be like other girls...

My claim that I'd gotten a Barbie for Christmas, but wasn't allowed to bring her to school, was met with scepticism. Sara-Lynn Brock, the leader of that exclusive pack, called me a liar outright. "You're just saying that so you can play with us," she said, with a characteristic toss of her long, shiny blue-black hair. "Prove it!" she said.

So early that spring, before the snow had melted entirely, I hatched a plan to smuggle Barbie along to school.

Getting her there was easy: she rode under my coat until I got on the bus, where she was transferred to my lunch pail.

For a day or two I played under the stairs with Barbie and the other girls; I don't remember the specific reason my Barbie and I were ousted, but soon I was alone at the swings again, or off at

The Long Way Home

the forbidden frog pond with the boys. And Barbie lay in my desk, along with petrified orange peels and the moldy cracked-wheat crusts of countless meat-spread sandwiches.

Once it became apparent that she wouldn't change my life, I knew I'd have to sneak her back home. Had Barbie been the savior I'd anticipated, perhaps I'd have defied my parents forever: but she didn't help me make friends. So Barbie needed to be safely returned to my bedroom closet before Mom and Dad ever found out she'd been gone.

The original plan was to sneak her back into the house on a Thursday afternoon, when they'd be at the Dominion store in Niagara Falls until well after we got home from school. Every second Thursday was Dad's payday—grocery day. That's how it should have gone.

So Barbie went into my brown Yogi Bear lunch pail on a Thursday after school. The school bus dropped me off half a mile from our house; a providential bend in the road allowed a clear view past Arlen Keller's big milk barn and a fallow field, all the way to our driveway. And there sat our car, hard evidence that Mom and Dad had suddenly changed their long habit. Too frightened to think straight, I slipped into the woods beside the big creek and stuffed Barbie into a hollow log, swearing Lou to secrecy. I intended to rescue her as soon as opportunity allowed.

Every Thursday afternoon—soon every weekday afternoon—I got off the bus hopeful, but every day the car sat in the driveway as smugly as a tattletale waiting for the ripest moment. I daren't try to sneak Barbie in while they were home.

Barbie lay entombed in her log all that long mercurial spring. It froze and thawed; there was a late March blizzard, there were April downpours, and there was muck. It was Lou who finally spilled the beans: but after all, she owed me. Lou had been ditching her medicine—antibiotics for a serious kidney infection—and I had told on her.

The whole story was not heard: I didn't get to tell about how lonely I felt at school, how Barbie was going to help me make friends. My parents didn't know that was the only reason I'd clamoured for a Barbie doll in the first place. Their only concern was that I'd taken her to school against their edict. Maybe it was too painful for them to look at my social failure. They weren't able to extend me any grace that acknowledged my misery, not even the cold comfort of "We understand, but…" I don't remember Mom's reaction, but all of Dad's focus was on the perceived insult to my grandmother.

He drove me up the road to the bus stop to fish poor mouldering Barbie out of her log. Her platinum blonde nylon hair was full of leaf mulch, and most of her clothes had rotted off. I was given the choice of either a 'spanking', or driving out to my grandmother's house to tell her in person that I had so little regard for her that I had thrown her gift away. Dad's ritualistic discipline was brutal and humiliating; 'The Belt' was to be avoided at any cost.

Though I knew I should have obeyed my parents, my father's mercilessness hardened my heart. I could not bring myself to accept another beating, not even to spare my grandmother's feelings, so we drove to Niagara Falls through the rainy April night and picked her up. I sat alone in the dark back seat and mumbled insincere responses as my father told on me. The marvel of having Grandma Adamson in our car was some distraction from the bitterness of the situation. Inside me, the truth screamed—I only wanted to be part of something, I only wanted to make friends.

But it hadn't worked, and there were no mitigating circumstances. Mom and Dad thought the worst of me, and I'd opted to hurt my grandmother to save myself. Maybe I really was the cold and ungrateful monster they believed me to be.

That night as I lay in bed, a loud, persistent buzzing sound insulated me from feelings so strong they should have made me vomit. Cold relief that I'd escaped one of Dad's dreadful punishments alternated with anger as hot as lava around my heart. The closer I moved to the buzzing sound, the louder it got; the bitter, sharp feelings seemed to recede. I made myself smaller, to get even further away from the churning sickness, and curled up very hard and tight in the middle of that anaesthetic buzzing. Soon I couldn't feel anything at all.

CHAPTER 10

Marsh Road School was full of lessons, good ones and bad ones.

I learned three things during my third grade year there: I learned that I could take that buzzing sound with me anywhere, and that if I pulled it close enough around me, it could muffle hurtful words. I learned that the wooded gully down to the big creek beside the bus stop was a great place to spend the day if I wanted to avoid going to school. And I learned that I was not, after all, completely unworthy of friendship.

Miss Lamb, my grade three teacher at Marsh Road School, inadvertently led to my discovering that I could skip school. She introduced the class to blank verse with a poem called *Spring Is...* We were supposed to memorize it, but some glitch of cognition rendered it as nonsensical to me as a foreign language. *The Cremation of Sam McGee*, and nearly all of the poems in my *Child's Garden of Verses* wait as patiently in memory as real books on an actual shelf, their printed words still ready to be read from the insides of my eyelids. Because they told their stories with rhythm and rhyme, they were easy to memorize.

But when my turn came to recite *Spring Is...* I could only shake my head. Miss Lamb determined that if I wrote the poem out, I'd learn it. Dutifully I copied it, but only onto the sheet of foolscap; it wouldn't stay in my head. She increased my sentence. By the time she finally gave up on me, I was supposed to have written that poem out ten times. I got three pages done, and then decided I'd stop going to school, instead. To this day, all I remember is the title, followed by those three cryptic little dots: *Spring Is...* I know that Miss Lamb wasn't intentionally unkind; she tried, in the only way she knew, to warn me of the perils of laziness, of shoddy work habits. "You are going to grow up to be a hippie on the streets of Toronto," she once told me.

Well, I didn't, quite—but I did learn that since I could see the school bus coming long before Mr. Edwards the bus driver could see me, there was plenty of time to zip across the road, scramble down the bank, and hide in the woods. Liza had graduated, and Lou was sick a lot that year; so when I found myself fortuitously alone at the bus stop, I played by the big creek all day, ate my lunch when I got hungry, and simply walked home after the bus went past my stop again in the afternoon. Every eight-year-old country kid knows that real spring in the woods is better than paper spring in a poem. Several pleasant green and blue days passed before my parents got the inevitable phone call. After that, I relied on fake illnesses to avoid school.

A few years later, grade six, with my hair filthy and matted to dreadlocks, I sat on the afternoon school bus and swallowed air to stop the rumbling of hunger in my stomach. I stared out the window and made myself blind to everything but the beauty of the countryside rolling past. By then the art of selective hearing had matured to a true discipline. The weird kid I had become turned the buzzing up louder and louder and stared more and more intently out the window. But "Hey ugly!" still got in sometimes, along with Fleabag and Bucky Beaver. Kicks still connected and hurt, too.

Late into moonlit nights I sat up in bed and escaped into books. That was the year I modelled my stoicism on the canine protagonists of the novels I read and re-read: intelligent, self-sufficient loners, survivors. "I am a wolf," I said to myself. "I am alone and strong; I will not acknowledge hunger." That's what I told myself; and it worked. I didn't need a light to read by, I didn't need more food, and I didn't need friends or kindness. I ate air and listened to the buzzing in my head. And I allowed myself to daydream away into the woods.

By my grade six year, some of the philosophies of the sixties had filtered down to influence elementary school teaching practises. My forward-thinking teacher brought relaxation techniques based on transcendental meditation into her classroom. And she tried out some earnest social experiments on us, no doubt designed to foster introspection in her charges. As a kid who spent most of her time alone, introspection was as natural as breathing to me. I usually used moments of self-reflection to try to figure out what was wrong with me.

In one memorable grade six experiment, each student took a turn sitting at the front of the classroom, facing the blackboard, eyes closed. The rest of the class came forward, one by one, and demonstrated how he or she felt about the kid in the hot seat. A hard push on the shoulder indicated dislike; a pat on the head was neutral, a soft stroke to the cheek showed caring or friendship, and a two-handed caress meant you were really special to somebody.

When my turn came, I was resigned: I didn't expect more than a few pats on the head, and probably one soft pet from my good and loyal friend Tracey. Mostly I expected the hard push to my shoulder, and that's what I got, along with a couple of nearly injurious double-shoulder shoves from boys who wanted me to know just how thoroughly I was despised. One boy, who'd never before been overtly unkind, took the opportunity to try to rake his fingers through my matted hair as I sat there. My head was yanked back hard, and I heard "Fleabag!" and "filthy" hissed among the general titters.

So I was abashed to feel a lovely, deliberate, two-handed caress; and when my bemused classmates told me later who'd bestowed it, I didn't quite dare believe.

Stanley and I had been special to one another since the beginning of grade three. We met on the playground, became fast friends, and couldn't stop talking once recess was over. Miss Lamb gave us the option of either standing together, or sitting crammed together in the same desk for the rest of the day. It was Stan who answered that we'd rather sit together, and I knew he wasn't thinking of the discomfort of standing all day. Sitting together, we'd be even closer.

There was nothing cool about Stanley. He was the smartest boy in the class; his writing was illegible, and though he was clean, he always looked rumpled. Stanley brought salt kippers to school in his lunch every day, and always gave them to me. He had uncommon integrity for a kid: he never called me an unkind name. There was something special about him: he'd found his niche, and he had the respect of everybody in the class. He seemed never to have suffered for his open affection for me, and I never got over my crush on him. Stanley's presence made the general ugliness of elementary school bearable.

Mrs. Osborne, the grade six teacher of the social experiments, sent me out of the class one day—I don't remember why—and then told Stan that he had her permission to "knock her buck teeth right down her throat" if I kept 'bugging' him... I must've been bugging him: but I wonder what Mrs. Osborne thought of Stan's candid declaration that day?

There must have been *something* really insufferable about me: certainly I was a good example of social maladjustment, but Stanley never complained, at least not to me, and there'd have been no shortage of kids wanting to let me know that Stanley hated me, too.

Sometimes I still catch myself wondering what it was about me that seemed to make other people so mad.

Mrs. Osborne was a popular teacher. She frightened us for the first week or two of our grade six year—she was forceful, large, and a bit sloppy—always a bra strap slipping down, and hair that looked like she'd just come in from a windstorm. A battle-axe, somebody called her. But she treated us like kids who were maturing, and the class responded collectively by trying to live up to her expectations.

I, however, was well on my way to fulfilling all the terrible prophesies the world had dealt and I'd taken on faith. I was too young to be a hippie in Toronto, but I was an unkempt, unwashed girl with bad breath, few friends, and fewer hopes. Remembering, I wonder how I survived: for decades it took only cataloguing some of the old names to summon the leaden ball of anxiety in the pit of my stomach, the cold, sinister buzz inside my head. Most days the only haven was the friendly green and brown countryside, experienced vicariously through the school bus window. How I yearned to disappear among those soothing maternal hills.

There was a boy in my class who suffered as badly as I did. As far as I could see, his only sin was that his parents sent him to school dressed as a perfect little English schoolboy. For grade one picture day he wore a blue suit, complete with short pants, vest, penny loafers, and bowtie. Dickey wasn't a rough and tumble boy, but he probably wasn't the sissy he was labelled, either. I wonder if he ever got the chance to find out. He was even ridiculed by some of the teachers. Our grade five teacher, Mr. Frost, called him Sally. I wish I could say I'd befriended Dickey, but the truth is that I was glad the hatred was spread around a bit. Maybe Dickey felt the same way about me...

I'm sorry for the part I played in his humiliation one day. I was so relieved that I wasn't the butt of the incident, and so happy to be included in something, that I savagely smothered the outraged screams of my heart on his behalf. Personal integrity wasn't one of my strengths.

Cook's Mills School didn't have a lunchroom. We ate our lunches in the classroom, and weather permitting, went outside to play afterward. Most days everybody knew what everybody else was having for lunch. Tracey brought Campbell's tomato soup in a blue Thermos every day, along with a Sunkist orange the size of a softball. Stanley always had his salty little dried kippers.

I don't remember whose idea it was to replace Dickey's cookies with dog biscuits. Nearly the whole class conspired: a week's worth of impressive strategy went into making it all work. One kid brought a couple of dog biscuits, another brought raisins, there was cinnamon, there were chocolate chips; the dog treats were moistened, mixed with the other ingredients, and shaped. Somebody took them home and re-baked them. The end result was three credible-looking cookies, which were first admired, then wrapped in a twist of waxed paper. It wasn't too difficult to sneak the dog food cookies into Dickey's lunch pail. And the whole class, including me, waited with stifled snorts as he tucked into his lunch.

Dickey was not entirely unsuspecting. He wasn't a stupid boy, and some of the kids had been too obvious with their snickers of anticipation. He knew something was up; he was probably taken aback by the solicitousness of classmates who suddenly wanted to know how he was enjoying his lunch, and whether he had any cookies. He was used to overt nastiness: perhaps he didn't know how to react to more subtle mockery. At any rate, it was only after some prompting that Dickey bit into the doctored cookie. The rest of the class dissolved in raucous laughter as he raced to the front of the classroom to spit the mess into the waste basket.

He never retaliated, or even whined, that I recall. Was his home a serene place where he found sanctuary as a child, or did Dickey lay in his bed some nights with tears of hurt and rage leaking into his ears? Did he imagine the vengeance he'd wreak upon his tormentors some day, like I did—feel glorious, heady victory as the enemy lay mashed and bloody on the floor, stomped to never-having-been? Were there nights he imagined how he could change himself, somehow make people like him? (Talia Merrick, whom everybody called Tally; her mother ran the little country store where I spent any money that came my way. Tally was the only girl close to my age within bike-riding distance, but she was popular. On the school bus one late spring morning, grade three: "Watch this: I can make Rainie do anything—Rainie, take your top off. Look at her! What an idiot!" Oh yes, I knew there was something wrong with that—but maybe people would like me if I pleased them.)

I hope Dickey enjoys huge success as an adult, that he didn't spend too much of his childhood trapped inside the same cold dark buzz that I lived in. I hope he found The Way out and beyond. And if he has children of his own, I hope he's very careful about how they're dressed for school.

Grade six eclipsed even grade three in misery: it was the year Napper died, the year Mom finally cut my hair off close to my scalp because there was no longer any hope of getting a brush through it. It was the year Dad chaperoned a class trip to Pearson Airport -Toronto International back then—and a classmate warned him, "Just so you know, Mr. Adamson, nobody likes Lorraine." I can't imagine what my poor father must've felt, or remember how he answered. The next day at school, some boys wondered aloud how I could be such a loser when my dad was so cool.

But it was also the year I discovered that I wasn't quite powerless. One morning, something happened, and I beat up the school bus bully during the ride to school.

George and Joanie started kindergarten that year. They were very cute, and for a little while I basked in their reflected glory. My classmates had the power to make their school experience as miserable as mine, so I felt an immense and perverse gratitude when the twins' reception was based on their cuteness and novelty, rather than their relationship to me. "They're so perfect," cooed the girls in my class. "It's too bad they have you for a sister." It was too late for Lou, but I was hugely relieved that the twins hadn't inherited my curse.

Billy Warder's ugliness might not have been intended for them that winter morning. He was likely trying to get to me; and all he did, after all, was snatch their toques off their heads. It was a standard school-bus bully game: up and down the length of the bus, and back and forth across the aisle the knitted hats would go, with the twins, small and powerless, desperately trying to pluck them out of the air as they sailed just out of reach overhead. "Give them back!" they yelled, laughing, too young and green to fully understand they were being bullied, maybe thinking this was a kind of big-kid game.

And that would be that. They might get their toques back, trampled, wet, and soiled, by the time the bus pulled into the school driveway, but tomorrow it would be their lunches, and the next day it might be a kick or pulled hair, or an icy snowball smashing into the backs of their necks. Finally they would lose their names: instead of George and Joanie they would be 'Fleabag' and 'Contaminated'. Their fates would be sealed. The thought of my dear little brother and sister enduring that abuse was unbearable.

An enormous, unquenchable rage overtook me.

Billy ran his campaign from the seat directly behind mine. I stood up and turned around, my customary fear flown far away in the face of an anger fuelled by years of swallowed insults. I grabbed Billy by his coat collar with one hand, and mashed him down hard into the cracked and duct-taped green vinyl seat. My other hand became a lumpy, mean little fist, and with a passion that utterly swamped my lack of technique, I hammered the top of Billy's head. Four words growled out of my mouth: "*You—leave—them—alone!*" I pounded until his surprised and frightened voice broke through the roaring in my head. "Okay, okay, whoa...!" There were tears in his eyes.

I let go, turned around, and sat quickly down in my seat. I couldn't hear anything but the roaring in my head, much louder and hotter than the usual cold buzzing. I thought my heart might pound its way right out of my chest.

Looking up, I caught Mr. Edwards' eye in the rear-view mirror, and I knew that he'd seen it all. Fear bloomed huge and black—Billy would kill me at the first opportunity, and I'd be in trouble with the principal as soon as she heard from Mr. Edwards. Worse, trouble at school meant bigger trouble at home.

For a week I kept myself even smaller and quieter than usual, but the call to the principal's office never came. Mr. Edwards *had* witnessed the whole thing; I saw the fact of his knowledge on his face. His deep-set brown eyes never missed anything that went on aboard his school bus. But he didn't report me. And Billy Warder never bothered any of us again.

I wonder how things might have gone had I learned from that lesson.

But I didn't; relief overwhelmed all else. The whole incident blew over without anything terrible happening to me or my siblings, and that was enough for me. You can get quite a lot of mileage out of relief when your usual milieu is fear.

CHAPTER 11

It was just about a year later that we arrived from school one day to find the car running in the driveway, Mom at the wheel. "Get in," she said, and her dark eyes flashed with intent, with unspoken promises. "We're leaving." We didn't even go into the house.

I knew what we were leaving: we were leaving behind the smell of empty bottles, and the sight of a kitten's convulsively pedalling hind legs as it kicked its baby way out of life after being run over in our driveway one beery summer afternoon. We were leaving the shouting and swearing that made it hard to sleep at night. We were leaving Dad and his friends, with their bewildering secret embraces. We were leaving behind forever the belt, and fear, and shame. We were leaving Bucky Beaver and Fleabag and dead Napper. We were leaving, and we were never, *ever*, going back.

But, oh—weren't we leaving some goodness behind, too? Dad wasn't *just* a monster—he was our good dad, too. Though he loved us imperfectly, he also gave us treasures. There were things that made us family, things that wouldn't work without all of us together... How could we have story-times without Dad? They both read aloud to us; Mom read with wonderful expression, from the *Just Mary* books she'd kept from her own childhood. We clamoured for our bedtime favorites, *Kitty Crooked Crown* and *Orville Bug*. But Dad enchanted us all with *The Hobbit*, and the whole *Lord of the Rings* trilogy. Rapt, we sat in that magic listening circle, and Dad read us full of inspiration for a thousand kid adventures.

And before he gave his summers away to booze and bad friends, Dad was a necessary part of family daytrips to Dufferin Islands. Everybody would be there—all six of us, as well as Grandma and Grandpa, and most of the aunts and uncles and cousins. We crammed seatbelt-less and squirming into the sticky car, and nobody fought, because we knew we were going to Duff. Down in that dappled leafy hollow, the cool air smelled mossy and fresh, and soon we'd be laughing and splashing with cousins under the cold green dome of a waterfall. The grown-ups even took turns swimming—we could count on Dad to join us under the falls for a while. There were usually a couple of Hibachis going, and always a giant watermelon. Grandma warned us not to swallow the seeds; we weren't sure she was joking when she said they'd sprout in our stomachs.

Going home would be mellow; Dufferin Islands was right beside Queen Victoria Park, but you could get there without braving the Niagara Parkway. We'd all be cooled off and pleasantly tired, as relaxed as the long shadows that sprawled across our yard in the golden afternoon light when we pulled into the driveway. Napper danced and pranced around us as we got out of the car, jumping up to lick our sweaty faces in welcome-home greeting.

We were leaving those good summer days at Dufferin Islands behind, forever. We were leaving part of the future behind, too, the part where we remember those old days along with our father, for the children that should call him Grandpa.

But for years the grimy memory of old wounds made it easy to stay away. Easy to turn your back if you convince yourself there was never anything good or beautiful back there. Do diamonds always have to come out of a black pit? And after all, what could I possibly hope to gain by going back now? (My children need to know there *are* diamonds; and now that I'm not alone, I can go back and get them. The pit isn't so scary; Light overcomes the darkness. 'Though I walk through the valley of the shadow of death, I will fear no evil...')

"Where are we going?" somebody asked, maybe me, as we piled into the car. And when Mom said "Grandma's," my heart leaped. I looked at the twins, soon to turn seven, chattering happily about school. But Lou, just past her eleventh birthday, sat with silent tears tracking her face. Maybe her heart was softer than mine, fuller of the stuff that lets you forgive and not come easily unstuck from your family. Or maybe, being younger, she hadn't seen and heard all the things I had. But I didn't cry: I was glad, glad, glad. "Yes! Thank you!" I wanted to shriek. Something in the back of my brain marvelled at the hard, bright buoyancy of my heart. Something knew that I should feel like weeping, too.

It shouldn't be that easy to let people go. How can you know, when you separate so carelessly, that someday, when you've finally come to see your own frailty, you'll forgive theirs, and want to hold them again? A heart must be tenderized, broken: finally I can cry the tears that my thirteen year old self could not.

We talked about it that night in the spare room upstairs at Grandma and Grandpa's house, where Lou and I slept side by side in a nest of blankets on the floor. I was not sad, but Lou cried and asked, didn't I feel sorry for Dad? But I didn't. Inside me was a secret: there was danger back there, a poisonous lie about love and honesty that meant to destroy us all. Something about Dad's relationship with Marley being about integrity and love—even though it had to be kept secret. Something about the belt being for my own good, that his unwholesome beatings hurt Dad more than they hurt me, that he was only doing this because he loved me. Lies that were so sinister because they were founded upon a germ of truth, told by a man who believed them... It's easy for a lie to get in and stay for a long, long time if it rides upon the back of a truth.

We stayed at Grandma and Grandpa's house, the five of us, for a little over four months.

Mom worked her night job at Zeller's and looked for a new home for us by day. We got rides back and forth to school in Mom's or Grandpa's car. We didn't see Dad for some time, and I didn't miss him. I didn't miss him for years and years and years.

Grandma and Grandpa wrapped us deeply into the bosom of their home; they bound up our wounded hearts with practical care: good food and freedom from debauchery enveloped in the mellow glow of big windows and burnished hardwood floors. George and Joanie turned seven there, and Grandma made them a magazine-cover cake.

It was a time of healing for us: we got what our mother knew we needed—home and haven while she regrouped. We got dresses, Lou and I, for our school dances. Mine was created for my grade seven Christmas dance, the closest I ever got to a prom. The dresses, made by our fairy grandmother, were confections as sugar-spun and marvellous as the twins' birthday cake. There were matching evening bags and dancing slippers—my gown was palest pink, covered in little raised velvet flowers, deeper pink; the hem, square neckline, and angel sleeves bordered with velvet ribbon as soft and color-sated as the heart of a rose. Lou's dress was even lovelier, a delicate cloud of diaphanous yellow, sprigged with tiny green rosebuds. With her pixie face, pale olive skin and shining dark curls she looked like a Celtic water sprite, hand-maiden to the May Queen, as delightful as an April sunbeam in a secret grove.

I was not an awkward, gangly thirteen-year-old in my dress. Grandma, with her seeing eyes, knew that inside the clumsy, long-legged lank-haired swatch of twitching nerves a tall and almost graceful young woman was poised to emerge. Grandma the chrysalis weaver wrapped me in and coaxed me out.

I went off to my Christmas dance knowing that I'd be hatefully mocked because of my beautiful dress. Everybody else would be wearing their best jeans, or the clothes they wore to church. I would be the only real princess there, and I'd sit alone against the gym wall all evening. The cool kids would smirk and make rude comments. But something in my girl heart knew that the love and care Grandma had worked into that dress must be honored, and I wore it regally, defiantly.

Something happened: nobody laughed. Some of the girls and a few teachers commented on how nice I looked. I even danced. Stanley was there—I hope I danced with him, but I don't remember.

Christmas came and went at Grandma's house, and then one day in the middle of spring break Mom announced we were moving. My aunt, on a country-road ramble, had found us a house to rent.

In January we went to school with the kids we'd known all our lives, and by March we were at a new school. I know there must have been a transition, some chance to say goodbye to Tracey and Stan—I know there must have been, for Tracey and I exchanged letters for a year or two.

But that interval is lost in the greater experience of our move.

Our new home was a revelation. My whole life had been lived in ignorance within twenty miles of extraordinary pastoral beauty. The voluptuous, rolling countryside, though tattered and grubby in the midst of a February thaw, enchanted my heart. So many lovely round hills, each with its little hollow. So many new woods to explore...

There were farms and fences, sturdy, gracious old houses, apple orchards with horses, pastures with contented Holsteins, and vineyards with foxes. There was a hundred-year-old stone gristmill with a waterfall and a millrace. There was even a lake. It was a bountiful land; around every bend in the road there was a vista like a blessing.

And there was the house.

It stood on the crest of a hill surrounded by mature hemlock trees, a big, matronly white clapboard farmhouse just beginning to settle comfortably into its final dilapidation. Its unpaved road was a pocked and dusty line that went steeply up hill and down dale between woods and wheat fields. Our new driveway was a quarter-mile stretch of axle-breaking hard-packed dirt, as full of potholes as the road. It went past our new house and made a farmyard loop which brought it by several outbuildings and the hired man's house before finally stopping back at the kitchen porch in front of the main farmhouse, *our* house.

This was where we were going to live. Our house was nearly a hundred years old, built by a prosperous dairy farmer around the turn of the last century. It had three porches—one at the front kitchen door, another at the back kitchen door, and a third—a small, dainty, formal porch at the official front door. The kitchen porch was supported by shapely wooden columns; under the eaves of the formal porch there was gingerbread. The back kitchen porch was open to the sky; it wasn't fancy, but there was the added bonus of a well with an old-fashioned hand pump just a few steps into the yard. Thankfully, because the water in the house was undrinkable, yellow and stinking of sulphur.

Indoor plumbing and push-button light switches were state-of-the-art modern conveniences when our house was built. A long-disused outhouse still stood halfway between the milk barn and the house, a practicality left over from the days when housework meant scrubbing floors regularly. After the morning milking, when the farmer and hired hands came in for breakfast, there would be no trekking loose, manure-smelling hay through the house and up the stairs to the only bathroom.

In the house, there was a cold pantry, back kitchen stairs, and a formal front staircase with a long, smooth oaken banister. A bald-headed newel post stood sentinel at the bottom of the stairs, as straight and patient as a butler. One of us named it. The formal dining room featured a plaster bas relief ceiling; there was a den; sliding oak doors separated the dining room from the large living room, the living room from the central hallway and front stairs. There was a stove-pipe hole in the kitchen ceiling, and a *maid's room* at the top of the back kitchen stairs. There were many, many windows, and every one stretched from just above the floor, all the way up to the eleven-foot ceilings. It was a house full of light and air.

CHAPTER 12

My transformation began soon after our move. Our house had room enough for every big idea, every dream. It was big enough for growing children, big enough to let all of us stand up, yell, sing and dance, without fear of being knocked down. How brave and full of faith she was, to try to give us that place of peace. We belonged there; I thought it would be our home forever. The farmhouse enfolded me as lovingly as an old dream of comfort—a dream older than the womb. Perhaps it was the comfort of freedom from sticks and stones and wounding words at school, or the delirious luxury of having Mom's attention and encouragement again. Perhaps it was gratitude for all the fresh, new beauty in our lives: the countryside surrounding us, the family nest where I knew we were truly safe at last, and loved. Perhaps something about the farmhouse was so like Home that my spirit responded in a joy of recognition.

Maybe it was just blissful ignorance of the calm before the storm.

The house had been empty for some time. It was old and elegant, but, insulated only by its grove of hemlocks, it was also drafty and cold. There were black oil stains on the living room floor where a previous tenant had torn a car motor apart, and the back kitchen stairwell was smeared floor to ceiling with greasy soot. A seven foot crack ran up the plaster of one living room wall.

All of the oak had been painted over—the crown molding around the windows and doorways, the wainscoting and sliding doors, the built-in corner cupboard in the kitchen, even the banister and newel post. Much of it was peeling. Honeybees had nested in one of the chimneys; their sleepy summer smell perfumed the upstairs bedrooms.

Hours and days were spent polishing the tarnished old brass kitchen faucets, scrubbing rusty hard water stains out of the bathtub and toilet. Furniture came from Grandma and Grandpa, Aunts and Uncles, and assorted other family; for the first time we each had our own bedroom. The den got furnished somehow, and after we'd been there a few months we inherited a television, which went into the gabled playroom upstairs. Artistic in everything, Mom was queen of eclectic shabby chic decades before it was legitimized by media home decor gurus. Somehow she made all the mismatched hand-me-downs work. Together we toiled and played, and brought the comfortable old wreck back to cheerful life.

That was when I began to try something different at my new school, where nobody knew me or my ugly nicknames. Deliberately, diligently, I observed and catalogued. Though still pale and skinny in ill-fitting second-hand clothes, I was clean and brushed, and finally confident enough to focus outward, to watch and listen. Like an undernourished stray that's lucked onto a kind master, I soon learned that making eye contact wasn't necessarily going to result in a curse or a kick. By the time grade eight finished, I'd even joined a fledgling after-school softball club. I was still very quiet and spent too much time staring out the school bus window, but I managed to fit in with a small group of girls over the next couple of years.

At home, I was getting to know my pretty and talented mother. I was proud of her courage and charisma, and as a young teenager I loved it when our new neighbors asked, "Which one's the mother and which is the daughter?" She often wore her dark hair in pigtails, and with her trim girlish figure, she really looked closer to twenty than thirty-five. I was honored to be her daughter, to brag about her talents.

One afternoon we arrived from school to find our beautiful old house dressed in wonderful, whimsical spring finery. In a single afternoon, on an ancient Singer sewing machine that was at least as ramshackle as the house, Mom had whipped up bright yellow Priscilla curtains for the big living and dining room windows. They were the color of French's prepared mustard, and should have been garish; instead they glorified the sunshine that poured through them.

Mom's curtains illuminated those rooms the same way her suddenly bright personality lit up our new lives. Her energy was boundless that first year: we'd come home from school to find she'd taken on and finished a new project almost every day—and then, if she didn't work that evening, we'd be outside exploring the fields and woods 'til suppertime, or off on a drive learning our new countryside. Home to eat—and after the dishes were done, maybe we'd be off again. Often she made a pot of coffee after supper, and I'd sit up with her in our living room, sometimes until dawn.

We were friends, Mom and I: it was very 'seventies'. I took advantage of my position as confidante, and missed school regularly. Mom enjoyed my company; we might spend the whole day on a long drive in the Southern Ontario countryside. She taught me to drive that year. I was only fourteen, but the country roads were nearly empty, and what if something had happened to her? She needed another driver in the house. So I learned to drive standard transmission on an old Vauxhall Epic Envoy bought for her by Grandma and Grandpa, the first of many calamitous vehicles she owned as a single parent.

How hard she must have fought against the fear, how frightening to contemplate the future. She was trying to raise four young kids on a minimum wage part-time job and Mother's Allowance, which was welfare for single moms. Mother's Allowance clawed back all but a fraction of what she earned, but we needed that fraction, and she had to commit to so many hours in order to keep the job. Dad was supposed to pay eighty dollars a month in child support—five dollars per kid per week, a sum which insulted me even then. Dad was a lab technician at a chemical abrasives factory; he had a good job, but an even better lawyer. His cheques, if they arrived at all, often bounced.

What a difficult place Mom was in: she used to tell me how guilty she felt, going to work and leaving me to look after the younger kids; and how guilty she'd have felt if she'd opted to stay home with us instead. Then there wouldn't have been enough of anything, and she'd have lost the shred of dignity afforded by staying off regular welfare. During our second year at the farmhouse, she took a journalism course at the local community college, one of her attempts to get some practical good from her gifts. By then I was in charge while she went to her night job at Zeller's. After getting the other kids into bed, I'd take my post at the tall narrow west window in the living room, where I'd watch for her headlights across the dark fields. She worked until nine and I'd agonize if she wasn't home by nine-thirty. Since it took forty-five minutes to close the store and drive home, I spent many anxious evenings waiting at the window.

It was shortly after we moved to the farmhouse that she 'met' Neil Diamond at work. His eyes, she said, followed her from his 'Moods' album cover in the Zeller's record department. Mom resisted as long as she could, and bought the record a few weeks later. Around the same time, spring 1973, odd things seemed to be happening in our house; sometimes we smelled orange blossoms, but the nearest orange tree was thousands of miles away. Doors were very accommodating, opening or closing by themselves when our arms were full of laundry baskets or groceries, and the swivel rocker in the living room—Mom's chair—rocked even when it was empty. At first Mom said the house was haunted by a 'good ghost', but soon it was clear to her that the 'ghost' was Neil Diamond, and that he was using his God-given telepathic and telekinetic gifts to communicate with her.

Richard Bach ushered the New Age into our home with his wildly popular novel, 'Jonathan Livingston Seagull'. It became our bible, and we dove greedily into its seductive gospel of self-actualization. It validated Mom's belief in freedom of the self as the highest expression of the divine. It told me there was hope, that if only I remained true to myself, I might someday rise above my circumstances. I felt superior, light years ahead of my giggling boy-crazy peers, one of the chosen few who got it. Neil Diamond's movie soundtrack gave us beautiful music and illumination for the novel. For a while, Mom was in telepathic communication with Richard Bach, too.

We'd sit drinking strong coffee in the twilit living room, her and me, and speak reverently of God and time and love. "Look," she'd say, pointing, "Do you see the stars?" I'd look up into the dim ceiling corners, and yes, I *did* see stars, a haze or mist of tiny playful sparks twinkling in and out. You could only see them if you didn't look directly. *What were they?* Could they have been manifestations of spiritual beings? Or were they just the sad symptoms of mental illness, figments of Mom's hectic imagination? If that was all, why did I see them too? I *did* see them—didn't I?

And I sat in Mom's chair, the one that seemed to rock all by itself, and felt comfort, a protective, embracing presence. I smelled the flowers all through our house.

Or did any of it really happen?

Something was going on: but what? Was I simply so needy, so hungry for love and attention that I swallowed Mom's whole psychosis greedily? Was her personality so charismatic and powerful, and mine so small and timid, that I'd see and believe anything she showed me? But we needed a little magic, a little hope...

Isn't it ironic that now I believe in a God who tells me to live by faith, not by sight... Then, I believed my eyes; now I believe in that which I cannot see.

CHAPTER 13

Outdoors, we were country kids in a new land: a land of traipsing out to the farmyard in the evenings to fill a five gallon jug from the old-fashioned water pump between the big barn and the milk barn. The convenient well just outside the back door turned out to be dry, but the one between the barns—originally intended for watering livestock—was alive and gushed achingly cold, clear sweet water. That was our drinking water. Miraculously, we didn't contract some terrible old-fashioned water-borne disease.

It was a country where, after the water was brought in, there was still the trip to the orchard to be made, to choose apples or pears for our school lunches. Two hundred fruit trees had been allowed to go wild: mostly apples, but some pears, crab apples, and a few quinces. In the orchard, long grass lay flat and smooth under its own weight, and windfalls were beyond plentiful—late in summer, the chilly night air was cider-sharp with the scent of apples. Deer loved our retired orchard; we planted a big vegetable garden next to it that first spring, and they enjoyed our lettuce, too.

It was a country of sweet-smelling haylofts, of clambering onto the tin roof of the milk barn on a summer Saturday night, straining to see something more than headlights from the local stock-car track as they swept the lower sky. Far away and faint across the dusky hills we heard the engines buzz like disturbed wasps.

Mom readily shared in the fun of our new home. Our first summer there, she found a can of paint in a dusty corner of the tack room. It was a putrescent shade of green; with it she tricked out the derelict manure cart that ran on an elevated track around two sides of the big milk barn. The 'Doom Buggy', emblazoned with biliously grinning skull-and-crossbones, provided many hours of entertainment. And another mom might have been exasperated with the gore of crushed mulberries on kids and old sheets, but she only laughed, delighted by our grisly creativity. That was us: the laughing wounded. We were so fat on fun, we didn't know we were starving.

There were wonderful pranks and misadventures. A nice middle-aged couple lived across the lane, in the original farm's foreman's house. Caroline was a city girl, and had never outgrown her suspicion that vagrants and perhaps even werewolves lived in the woods, and came out to hunt at night. She was convinced, too, that their favorite prey was a lady alone. And Caroline's husband Henry often worked the night shift at the Nabisco plant in Niagara Falls.

Our creation was an awful thing to behold: Zombie Lady's noggin was a Styrofoam wig head impaled on a broomstick, with face painted on and marbles stuck into the eyeholes we'd gouged. A string mop for hair completed our creation, and finally a heavy brocade satin hooded cape, a gift to me from Grandma who had a flair for the dramatic, hid both the broomstick and the kid perpetrator of a terrible practical joke. We sneaked out into a wild and windy October night, a moon-shiny night of waving hemlocks, flying clouds, and rattling windows. It was a night we revelled in, country kids at home; but for poor Caroline it was a night for turning the TV up a little louder, maybe checking the clock a little more often.

Caroline's yard backed onto a slim belt of trees, her only protection from acres of dark forest and fields, prowling-room for all kinds of fearsome countryside monsters. But the monsters were much nearer than she imagined. One of them—Lou or a mischievous visiting cousin—scratched at her living-room window, skilfully random. Once, she doesn't really notice; twice, maybe she glances up from the hockey game. But the third time, she gets up, goes into the kitchen, bravely forces herself to open the back door.

And that's when I make my move, that's me under Zombie Lady's cape, rush-gliding across Caroline's backyard just outside the sharp rectangle of light on the dark grass. There's a shriek, a slam, we don't know what else, we're too busy running away, getting back into our own house, collapsing in hysterical laughter. Mom made us apologize in the morning.

There was the whiskey Lou and I made in the carriage shed. It started innocently enough, with an old oak rain barrel. Don't all kids make potions? When we were only five or six, we made poison-berry jam for my cousin's neighbor, Bonnie, who'd offended us somehow, probably just by being a year older, and so, insufferably, a year ahead of my cousin in school. We took an empty mason jar—sealers, Grandma called them—from a shelf in the utility room, and filled it with crushed honeysuckle and deadly nightshade berries. Poison-berry jam; fortunately, Bonnie wasn't buying it.

The barrel was full of mosquito larvae and stagnant rainwater that had leaked through the dilapidated roof. In the murky light at the back of the carriage shed, it managed to seem simultaneously crystal clear and deeply amber. Lou and I added a few apple cores, some wild grapes, handfuls of ripening wheat, and grass clippings; then we covered it with a handy plank. Our brew was as natural as maple syrup, and a lot less work. We looked in on it from time to time, and gave it a stir once in a while. Nothing much appeared to be happening, so we forgot about it; but Ontario August brought our concoction remarkably to life.

One thick afternoon, an exuberant, long-threatening storm broke, with sudden sheets of hard, warm rain, thunder and lightning, and finally, pebble-sized hailstones. Lou and I dashed from the dirt turnaround lane to the nearest shelter, which happened to be the carriage shed. We stood drenched and giggling, enjoying our respite from the daunting heat and humidity.

There came a noise from the back of the shed: "Glup." We turned to look, because 'glup' is neither an animal nor a human noise. 'Glup' is the sound made by a rubber boot fighting for its life against an eager, hungry cesspool of boggy muck. 'Glup' is a noxious sound, a swamp-gas sound, a creature-from-the-black-lagoon sound... And 'glup' was the sound emanating from our rain barrel. A vaguely green, frothy mass had bubbled powerfully up, forcing the lid askew; our witch's brew was getting out. It burbled and murmured, oozing and drooling over the rim of the barrel as though vomited. It smelled richly of grass clippings and other green decay. We didn't even dare one another to taste it.

◆

Mom knew you can't properly run a home without pets, so we acquired a cat. PC—Puddy Cat—an occasionally-slim calico who presented us with kittens so regularly that Mom joked her initials stood for 'Pregnant Cat'. PC started out as a housecat, and was relegated to the barn once her easy virtue became apparent. Mom couldn't afford to have her spayed, so there were always kittens around. The rule was only one kitty in the house; PC came in to eat, then back to the barn she went to look after her progeny. That worked, until one especially cold and snowy winter when we smuggled a young litter into the basement via the root cellar door, and planned to winter them there. Mom discovered our secret and sent them back to the barn, but the damage had already been done.

Maybe poor PC was confused, and had been trying to move her babies back to the relative warmth and sure food of the cellar. That was our surmise: either she'd been carrying them one by one over the deep snow in the lane, or they were trying to follow her back to the house. And Henry, good country neighbor that he was, had hooked the plough up to his truck to clear our lane and driveway. Sadly, two or three kittens were caught and buried in the snow banks thrown up by the plough. Of course they were smothered, or froze to death, which was bad enough; but somehow they got unearthed from the snow bank and ended up in the lane, and the little frozen bodies were subsequently run over, probably by our landlord, who stored hay in one of the barns and came regularly with tractor and wagon to take a load back for his dairy herd.

It was a sunny blue-and-white winter day, cold and clear, and we were on our way out to survey our domain after a week of snowstorms. How shocking and horrible, how heartbreaking, to discover the kittens silhouetted against the hard-packed snow of the lane like cardboard cut-outs. Then, macabre hilarity rising to do battle with tragedy, somebody yelled "Kitty Frisbees!" and suddenly there were George and Joanie, and maybe Lou, cart-wheeling the flattened little bodies back and forth across the lane.

No wonder we were nicknamed the Addams Family!

There were spring-times of virginal and imaginary girlish romance, of sitting in apple trees enthroned as a queen among bowers of sweet-smelling blossoms. There were rambles alone in the woods, quiet and companionable as Eve in the Garden with God. One summer, fifteen and limber, I climbed a tall beech tree beside a cow pond in the woods many times, and waited; within minutes, deer came back to drink. And there was once a bright May morning, when sprightly through a fallow field, I happened upon a sleeping fawn. He, still wobbly-young, scrambled blinking to his feet—I stopped dead, and we stood like that, nose to nose, until I put out my gentle hand for him to smell and he turned and bolted for mama. True; magical...

There was a summer night I clamoured to sleep in the hayloft, "please, please!" I'd always wanted to—something about the smell. Freight trains and haylofts: I never did get to hitch my ride on an overnight boxcar, but Mom let me, finally, spend the night in our hayloft. I talked Lou into joining me, and perhaps a neighbor kid or a cousin; we set up our sleeping bags or blankets in a nest of loose hay, and the dark, when it fell around us huge and soft, was full of the minute scratching and squeaking of scampering mice. I didn't care, but my company was frightened. We made a beeline for the house; Mom never really secured anything, but that night we found every door locked tight. I'm glad, because otherwise I wouldn't be able to say I've slept in a barn.

Every kid should be blessed with at least a year on a farm: we had three. Three summers, three barns; and a silo, a corn crib, a chicken coop, a carriage house, an outhouse, an orchard, and acres of woods, fields, and creeks.

When I talk about my childhood, I often say 'I grew up on a farm', but the truth is, Mom just rented an old farmhouse, and we only lived there three years. But those were three years of such fantastic growth, of fully awakening to the beauty of love and family, that when I think of home and childhood, the farmhouse comes first to mind. Those years were also full of secret sickness growing, of illness calling itself vitality. But I didn't know that for a long time.

CHAPTER 14

In retrospect the signs of bi-polar disorder were clear: those first couple of years after leaving Dad, she managed to hold a part-time job, go to college, keep our great big house spotlessly clean, and play wholeheartedly with her children. By herself she wallpapered the kitchen. She washed windows and made curtains and clothes. She painted a giant, ferociously optimistic daisy over the long crack in the living room wall. She planted and tended a vegetable garden. She hiked in the woods with us, collected wild ginger and candied it. The drives we took always became adventures: the rougher the road, the more likely she was to go that way. Once we travelled down a rutted muddy track that ended promisingly at a trail into unknown woods. She parked the car, and off we set; somehow we got lost. With dusk falling and the twins tearful and worried, we hiked our way home. The next day, she got her sister to drive around the countryside to find the car. She sketched and wrote and stayed up 'til daybreak. She laughed and sang, in love with life and hope. She was the best mother in the world—she drank down and relished each day with an exuberance that seemed holy to me, a gift from God.

I like an orderly home, but I've never been able to keep my house as clean as Mom kept hers. I can't make curtains, either, or anything else that requires a sewing machine, time, and ready inspiration. She did everything on the fly, and never landed before her project was complete. We were up in the clouds with her, and for a long time all we saw were silver linings.

The crash came, eventually—preceded by a long, steady arc. I tried to run fast away from it, desperately hanging onto love and beauty. I'd have run back in time, if possible, to the year or two we had Mom nearly all to ourselves, and I'd have stayed there longer. But the terrible progress of her illness outpaced my childhood; like inexorable lava down a mountainside, it destroyed everything in its path, and soon even beautiful Creation was not enough to save me, or any of us.

It started with automatic writing; she'd taken to sitting with her eyes closed, or staring at something an eternity away on the ceiling, with a notebook on her lap and a pen in her hand. Sometimes she'd stop after a few minutes, and there'd only be scribbles. But often she'd write for hours, and there would be many pages closely covered in confident, almost vertical, script. Her handwriting, usually so graceful and tidy, would be a masculine mess of frenetic creativity. That was when Neil Diamond was writing to her; she was recording his half of their conversation. As far as Mom was concerned, she was only holding the pen—he was doing the writing. Joyfully she shared their conversation with me; and because her joy was so genuine, I believed in its foundation with the whole faith of a new convert. Often she spoke out loud to him. I assumed comprehension, and so I understood too. But my own experience was much less concrete, more like the communication that occurs in dreams where you're surprised by your complete mastery of a foreign language. We were talking to *somebody*; if not Neil Diamond, who? Did those mystical thoughts and words just stick to the ceiling for a while, injuring my mother when they finally succumbed to the weight of their own deceit?

What an honor to be included. I was an initiate to the most intimate and magical circle imaginable, happy to finally belong to something bigger than myself. Overjoyed that I mattered to them—I was Mom's confidante, and Neil 'spoke' to me, too. Their affair coloured every aspect of our lives. For a few years it consumed me as thoroughly as it consumed her. I'd had a lot of practise living in my own head—Mom's psychosis created a rich new wonderland indeed. During the morning ride to school, I fantasized about the day Neil's limousine would overtake our school bus. He'd board the bus, and take us all away: my new, good father. Mom would already be there in the limo, waiting. We would never be poor again. That was it: happily ever after came next.

Recalling, I marvel again at my own survival: I walked with my mother into a dream, lived alongside her in an illness that produced feverish delirium. No drug could have conjured a more convincing hallucination. I believed, went with her deep into delusion. I sat with her late into summer nights, poring over the lyrics to the Neil Diamond 'Serenade' album, which seemed to confirm everything she believed. In hushed expectation and hope, I believed. Now I call it illness, and pretend to know what it was; I turn my eyes away from it, and focus, sometimes stubbornly, on the apparent dichotomy of following Christ.

But in those days I lived in it, and believed it was truth.

Occasionally I ask: how is my belief in the Person of Jesus now any different than my teenage belief in Mom's affair with Neil Diamond? Those lyrics *were* most compelling, when taken in context with everything else that seemed to be happening...

What if it was real? What if she really had some kind of psychic bond with Neil Diamond, a relationship as sacred and mysterious as marriage; and what if the 'illness' I so determinedly walked away from wasn't a psychosis, but something we saw and experienced with the eyes of our hearts? Was it so convincing because it was real, after all? Do my sisters and brother keep a secret vault, too, and still ask themselves sometimes, *was* it real? What if the condition we call bi-polar disorder isn't a sickness at all, but an unredeemed divine gift, the gift of prophecy, corrupted? Maybe that's why none of us has managed to live fully in the 'real' world. All those failed relationships, all the dropping out of school, the jobs that might have become successful careers, if only we weren't all trying to live with one foot still stuck in Mom's alternate reality... (Because what if—*what if*—Mom's reality was the *real* one?)

And me, the hedger of bets: did I finally just default to Christianity because I thought I could have both worlds, something mystical to hold the terror of great big practical eternity at bay, but still comfortingly normal? I need something to keep me far from Mom's craziness, but that something must still provide the fix of *otherness* her illness provided.

⁂

Though happiness and contentment marked those days for me forever, we were very poor. During the bus ride to school one day, I overheard a girl remark to her friend, "Did you see the way those skinny little Adamson kids attacked their lunch? They look they've never had a decent meal." She was talking about the twins. We *were* thin, all eyes and teeth and bony knees. And every morning on the bus, George and Joanie dug into their cookies with the greedy enthusiasm of children who'd never learned to take a treat for granted. My face burned with shame, and I tried not to hear the whispered "Shhhhh! Rainie's right there!" I didn't *feel* poor, but some days while we were at school, Mom went off into the woods to forage for food.

In a grade nine math class one day, I sat with elbows propped on my open text book, hands cupped around my eyes to mask my nap. And was waked by a vision as bright and tonic as a splash of cold champagne: suddenly, and for only a second, I was in the woods. It wasn't merely a momentary dream; I smelled it, felt the spongy ground, saw the scalloped, silver-green detail of tiny lichens on a twig amid the leafy debris at my feet. I 'woke' with a start, and stayed awake and fresh the rest of the day, though I'd probably been up late with Mom the night before. Home from school that day, I shared my marvellous experience with her; she revealed that she'd been in the woods herself that very afternoon, looking for food. The implication was that we had grown so close that I'd been transported, and somehow seen the woods through her eyes. Nothing like that has happened to me since; and it disturbed me that Mom tied it to her own experience, as though every good and magical thing necessarily had something to do with her. Perhaps it did; certainly that's what I believed in those days, and for many years after. Mom's charisma was like a drug.

So unworldly was I that I found nothing remarkable about our mother wandering around the springtime woods, looking for food like a fairy-tale parent.

One day my aunt got a call from the elementary school because George and Joanie had been going without lunches. Likely they'd been left behind in the fridge: I can't imagine Mom having forgotten something like that—certainly *I* had a lunch, and if I'd made it myself, I'd have made lunches for the rest of the kids, too. But our poverty must have been apparent enough to alert teachers. I do remember Grandma and Grandpa coming to our house with big boxes of groceries. But that's what you do, isn't it? You're supposed to help those who can't help themselves.

It was many years before I understood just how poor we were, compared to our peers, and just how ill Mom was. Many years went by before I realized that other kids went to the dentist, other kids went to summer camp and church, and other kids played sports and got music lessons. When I was older, an adult, I understood, and brought groceries for her, coffee and cigarettes and fifty bucks here and there. It was an honor to help her; she was my beautiful and brilliant mother, living in a world for which she was far too fragile, as pitifully ill-equipped as a butterfly in a blizzard.

By our second year at the farmhouse, something new was happening to Mom; the arc had reached its zenith and begun its inevitable decline; she was starting to act oddly. She'd go from vivaciously engaged to vacant zombie overnight. There were times she'd spend the whole day sitting at the dining room table writing madly, other days spent silently staring out the big living-room picture window from her swivel rocker.

Some evenings she'd disappear into her room right after supper, and we might not see her again until the next day. Our second Christmas at the farmhouse, she locked herself in her bedroom in the morning, and I banged on her door and pleaded with her to come out. There was a turmoil of fear and resentment inside me: "Mom, it's Christmas! I'll make some coffee. You have to come out! What about Lou and George and Joanie?" She was in there with her notebook and Neil, but my fourteen year old self knew that her children were supposed to come first, at least on Christmas Day. George and Joanie were only eight, little kids who still needed their mother along for Christmas morning. A kid that age needs Mom or Dad in a favorite chair with coffee; somebody big to shine their joy at, somebody to bear their gratitude as they dance all starry-eyed around the tree. What happens when a kid's heart gets too full? If nobody shares its sorrows and joys, does it eventually burst, and the wine or vinegar inside spill out all over everybody? What happens? (Tell somebody. Tell *Him*.)

There we were—children who still needed family and feasting, and real blessings in the land of the living. But our mother was being stolen away by a glamour so shiny we were fooled into following as though it really was light in the darkness.

Only Lou refused to join our dreamy pied-piper dance, but by then she had her own demons, and she needed attention. But Mom wasn't there: before our eyes she was sucked as dry as a scarecrow, and the sparkle that used to be so full of fun and promise was turning out to be the glitter of craziness.

Maybe I knew even then that she was sick beyond mere self-centredness, but oh, it was so much easier to stay fooled and keep the false joy, to lock that terrifying suspicion into a deep, dark corner, and do whatever I could to stay in the feverish light. It had become *my* light, too, something that seemed good and right, made me think deeply and experience feelings that finally went beyond personal hurt. For years it satisfied an inherent need for *story*; Mom's 'relationship' with Neil Diamond provided a fantastic, mythical and mystical framework upon which I could hang every blossoming romantic notion, every faltering grasp for meaning in a bewildering world.

Years later, decades later, I began to wonder whether, at some obscure level, she may have *chosen* to stay sick. If she did, I'm forced to ask why anybody would choose a dream over bracing, exhilarating, dizzying real life. What makes a person so satisfied with the fiction inside her head that she's incapable of joining the flesh-and-blood life going on around her? Is it a kind of immaturity, the self-centred attitude that your life belongs only to you, and if it doesn't go your way, you don't want any part of it? Maybe it was the only way she could exert some control over a life lived in response to breakneck circumstance.

If she *didn't* choose, what does that say about free will, about the character, perhaps even the very existence of the God I've placed my belief in...? After all, if God *really* cared the way a loving father should, wouldn't He have placed us all with the right people in the first place?

But of course now that I'm old and faithful, I know the answer to that question. The difference between my belief in Jesus and Mom's belief in Neil Diamond is a difference of foundations; it's the same *kind* of belief, and that's why it lasted so long, and why it usually felt so good and right. And because it was a belief founded upon an illusion, that's why it came with mystery, occlusion, and disquieting dreams. Fundamentally, it was the same kind of faith, but built on a lie, and therefore structurally unsound and doomed to fail.

But what about people like Mom? What if the only place you feel safe is the world you've built inside your own head? What if you're too fearful to leave that world—you *know* your world, it is home, but the world outside your head is a mystery. Fear, the roaring lion that cripples sanity, makes it impossible to get over the habit of living in fantasy instead of waking up to the awful, messed-up, loveable people you're stuck with here in the world. Fear that imprisons the mind and spirit in lonely hell, surrounded by imaginary people: maybe fear that you aren't as great as you're trying so hard to be; fear that others will reject you when they find out. Fear that real life might not turn out the way you imagined it—fear that you might fail. Maybe fear that you might succeed, that there is nothing bigger than you after all, no God who knows better than you: and that is too big a fear. That fear is bigger than anything else. So it's better, easier, to live in your head. Living alone is safer than anything else. Too bad you die at the end, anyway, just as if you had risked everything and lost—or won. Fear is boss of the one-man show. Maybe Mom's psychosis was just her inability or refusal to grow up and trust beyond fear; and the only comforting answer to that is the answer of grace.

Thankfully, that is a huge, resounding, and very comforting answer.

I try to make sure my kids know the truths I learned so late: they matter—not only to me, but to God, and so, ultimately, to the whole world. They believe, to varying degrees: one has swallowed the truth whole and experiences indigestion from time to time. He's growing, because truth is nourishment. One's picky, but I'm confident that since only the truth truly satisfies, that's what she'll ultimately turn to. And one is like a baby bird, needing his truth regurgitated, given and re-given in small and constant doses.

<hr />

So the farmhouse years were lived head-in-the-heavens, but the world caught up anyway. Beautiful, gracious old house: we lived like fallen aristocracy, starved and chilly in our castle. It was insulated by its protecting grove of old hemlocks, but nothing else. Atop a hill, with its rattle-trap, wavy-glassed windows facing the elements, it was impossible to heat. The furnace had been state-of-the-art around 1905, when it burned coal. At some point over the decades, it had been converted to an oil burner, and oil was gold in the early nineteen seventies. Mom was an automatic delivery customer—a big oil truck was supposed to show up about once a month to fill the great tank that squatted in our basement coal bin. Sometimes we ran out of oil before the truck arrived, and we'd spend a frosty few hours waiting. Occasionally that happened on a Friday afternoon, which meant we'd have to wait until Monday for our oil. We'd live in the kitchen and dining room those weekends, with the sliding doors closed, the upstairs sealed off, and the electric oven turned up as high as it would go. The kitchen had a stove-pipe hole, but unfortunately the wood stove was long gone. Cold, blustery winters sucked heat out of every crack and seam. The voracious old furnace lurked like a monster in its dark den: it guzzled oil, gobbled up money, and belched and farted inconsistent heat. Soon Mom owed the oil company more money than it was prepared to wait for. We had to move.

CHAPTER 15

Like our first move, it was halfway through the school-year, spring break. But I was nearly sixteen this time, in high school. I'd actually made friends: there were girls I gossiped with on the phone, in the hallways and lunchroom at school, girls I met at the skating rink on Saturday afternoons. We played crack-the-whip to get the attention of the pimply rink-rats we had crushes on, skinny adolescent boys who skated fast and furious, enforced the rules, and forbade 'crack-the-whip'. Your crush had real power and authority if he ran the Zamboni between skate sessions. Mom never seemed to mind driving me to the rink in town and picking me up a couple of hours later.

They were healing times: though I made no deep or lasting friendships, those girls mended the gaping hole rent by the social deficits of my elementary school years. They gave me companionship, laughter, shared girlhood.

There were glitches and hiccups of course; my social skills were still clumsy—for years I hung on to my grievance against the girl who'd made the starving twins remark, even though she had the courage to take me aside later that day and apologize. Perhaps I missed the opportunity to make a friend. And because I was no longer kicked and spat upon, I made the mistake of trusting every overture of friendliness, which set me up for some cruel pranks.

One day a popular boy hailed me from where he stood by his locker, surrounded by two or three of his goons. He used my real name—'Fleabag' and 'Bucky Beaver' were gone for good, but they'd been replaced by the more general 'Browner', reserved for us quiet, apparently studious types. But he didn't even call me 'Browner'. And because he used a sincere smile along with my name, I approached him. He apologized for bugging me—he'd been teasing me in a class we shared. It's just kidding around, he told me. "Friends?" he asked, holding out his hand and smiling. Wow, I thought to myself—this is what people do when they're growing up—this is really cool, I could be a part of it. So I smiled back, gullible me: "Sure, friends," and took his hand. Which he grabbed lightning-quick and pulled down to his crotch. Coarse laughter bellowed down the hall after me as I fled, feeling too shocked and stupid to do anything but escape. For a week "Friends?" seemed to mock from every bank of lockers, and taunt me and haunt me from every brainless little knot of jocks and slackers-to-be.

But overall, my first year and a half of high school had been a positive experience, and I'd learned a lot.

The girls I hung around with gave me a going-away card, and a small tin treasure chest full of caramels, which locked with a tiny, clever padlock and key. They wrote words of encouragement and reassurance on the card; it was good to feel liked and appreciated, though it didn't make moving away from my beloved farmhouse any easier.

We moved away from the hills and valleys, away from the woods and vineyards and waterfalls, away from the barns and orchards and pastures. We moved to a neighborhood in St. Catharines, a medium-sized city on the Welland Canal; apart from the few months we'd spent at Grandma and Grandpa's house, I'd never had a neighbor near enough to call 'next door'. We moved to a townhouse complex where we shared a wall with our next-door neighbor. It was social housing; a provincial government rent subsidy meant there'd finally be enough money for food *and* heat.

It was a street of dismayingly similar duplexes: red brick lower story, white clapboard second story. There were four bedrooms upstairs, and that was enough, because by then Lou had already been living with Dad in Niagara Falls for some time. She'd been exhibiting some troubling behaviour earlier that year – hiding in her darkened room and hoarding food while she pored over the "Man, Myth and Magic" magazines she'd somehow acquired. Under my self-absorbed adolescent radar, my coldly separated parents had come to a decision, and Lou had moved away from the farmhouse, away from Mom and Neil, and away from me and the twins.

Our tiny new backyard was separated from twenty identical others by a chain-link fence. The best thing about it was that it faced an open field which gave us a short-cut to the Welland Canal. Our backyard foliage was provided by a single scrawny Manitoba maple which seemed embarrassed by the dozen or so leaves it dropped every fall. We felt so sorry for it, so affronted by the dearth of shade and green, that Mom drove us to the Niagara Parkway that first autumn to collect garbage-bags full of bright October. Our neighbors raked in bemusement as we strewed an imported fall all over our pathetic little rectangle of grass. Mom was like that: she knew you could soothe heartache with silliness and autumn leaves.

The only way I could tell which house was ours, apart from reading the number, was by the colour of the front door. Some were red and some were dark blue. Ours was dark blue. We lived about two thirds of the way down the dead-end street we shared with our low-income neighbors. Within a week of our move, I'd gone into the wrong house twice after school.

There were many good things about our new neighborhood, but leaving the farmhouse grieved me as deeply as the breakdown of my family should have done, and I was incapable of recognizing any of them. Moving day I wept; I helped to wrestle furniture and load trucks, but I couldn't muster a smile even for the twins. All the way into St. Catharines in my uncle's truck, I cried and allowed nothing to comfort me. The house and hills were Home: so deeply rooted in my heart that moving away from them was like being orphaned.

I had no desire to adapt to city life; I'd never learned to ride a city bus, or cross a busy street. Walking on a sidewalk instead of in a ditch or along a gravel shoulder was a novelty. You cannot daydream your way along a city sidewalk: if you do, you'll bump into another pedestrian, or knock your brains out on a streetlight. Mom rode the bus with me to my new high school the first time to avoid a repeat of my grade one experience, when I got on the wrong bus after school. I was frightened by city traffic; Mom, mercifully and graciously unembarrassed by the timidity of her fifteen year old country-girl daughter, held my hand until I felt confident enough to cross the street alone. She met with my teachers, encouraged me as I made the midyear transition from a three-term school to a two-semester school.

The school building itself provided some comfort—it was very old. In my basement-level art class, exposed water pipes creaked and leaked. There were wide oak banisters which I slid down surreptitiously on a bathroom or fountain break during class, when I was certain nobody could see me. The building smelled old, felt old—not like our homogenous townhouse with its blue door and postage-stamp-sized yard.

Many things happened over the next few years.

Mom started work as a line cook at a downtown restaurant. Lou moved back in with us after a problematic several months with Dad. I don't remember whose bedroom she shared—probably Joanie's. At school, I made one good friend, got mostly acceptable grades, excelled in English, French, and art. Adventurous me, I joined the high school Outer's Club, went camping a couple of times, borrowed my cousin's ten-speed to bike across Manitoulin Island, went spelunking, learned to rappel. The Outer's Club was mainly comprised of science geeks and budding tree huggers, but it wasn't my social club—it was simply my means to an end: it got me out of town from time to time. I managed to navigate my new social circle fairly painlessly, but for me, 'out of town' really still meant 'away from people'.

Mom's affair with Neil continued; somehow she managed to buy concert tickets, and we saw his live shows at Maple Leaf Gardens in Toronto, and across the Niagara River at Buffalo Memorial Auditorium in New York. Over the years, I'd see many Neil Diamond concerts with my mother. Never once did I ask why she had to buy our tickets, just like the mere mortals who weren't Neil's soul mate. How could I? Asking that question would have meant acknowledging that perhaps their affair existed only in Mom's mind. Asking that question would have forced me to examine my own belief. So it hovered like a holograph in the periphery of my mind's eye, unacknowledged and unasked, for years. Sometimes when Mom was too broke to buy tickets, I bought them myself. More than once I paid scalper's prices, over a hundred dollars each. Still childlike in my belief, it never occurred to me to consider what bill might not get paid, or whether the twins might need shoes. Mom and Neil and their mysterious connection eclipsed everything else.

Georgie and Joanie and Lou went to the local elementary school; they made friends up and down our street. In the house, we became accustomed to hearing neighbors. The sound of singing birds was traded for urban noises: cars starting, doors slamming, neighbors talking and laughing, neighbors swearing and fighting, strident and beery. The opening riff to "Smoke on the Water", amped high and played over and over again, was permanently etched into our brains by the aspiring rock-star neighbor kid who lived in the other side of our townhouse. He never learned more than those iconic first couple of bars. AM radio scored the soundtrack to those times: I went to bed at night connected as if by an umbilicus to an earphone strung to a tiny transistor radio beneath my pillow. Every time a Neil Diamond song played, I woke up. I had become hard-wired to respond to his music; it would be decades before I realized there might be something unhealthy about that. My antenna is still up—it probably always will be.

I began to keep a journal, where I mainly recorded many wonderfully adventurous and vivid dreams. Most of my waking thought was still fixed faithfully around Mom and Neil; they were the centre from which all else radiated, and my unwavering focus on their star provided grist aplenty for dreams.

It was Neil Diamond who, in a dream, healed me of my inherited loathing of Americans. Of course, the truth is that it was dear God who spoke to me, God who is able to work through anything, even a psychosis, in order to implement His plans and purposes. In my dream, it was my birthday, and I was at a Neil Diamond concert. In fact, I *did* attend a Neil Diamond concert on my birthday one year. At the dream concert, he called me down onto the stage, wished me a happy birthday, and then took my hand. In an aside that was somehow kind despite its being amplified to reach twenty thousand people, he revealed that I hated Americans. Since the venue was Buffalo Memorial Auditorium, I was, of course, surrounded by Americans. There was a collective "awwwwww" of shocked sympathy from the crowd. Still holding my hand, Neil turned to me, smiling, and asked me whether his American hand felt any different than a Canadian hand. That was all; I woke with the truth installed and working. There was no residual emotional response, never a moment of catching myself in an old habit and having to remember I'd been cured.

My sixteenth year I got a summer job; I liked having money. From the earliest days of hearing my father lament, I'd wanted to work and help my family. Living in the country meant no paper route, of course—but from age eleven I scoured the classifieds anyway, and called every Mennonite farmer's ad for seasonal workers: grape pruners and fruit pickers. Mr. Neufeld, who grew grapes in St. David's or Vineland, chuckled and told me to call back when I turned thirteen.

After we moved to town, things were really hard for us for a while: Mom was doing free book-keeping for the local fuel company to pay off the enormous heating bill we'd run up at the farmhouse. She called her old landlord, a farmer, to see whether there was something I could do to help bring in a few more dollars for us. So I spent several nostalgic days back in my beloved fields, pruning and tying young grapevines.

Mom worked: two or three nights a week paying off the oil bill, and days at the restaurant. And later that summer I got a job at an old-fashioned corner grocery which also ran a lunch counter and ice-cream shop. After work, I watched the younger kids while Mom worked. But they weren't *well* watched; sometimes when I remember those years, it looks like we were all parentless kids, even Mom—a whole houseful of Pippi Longstockings.

The twins and I managed to find a naive balance within our family's dynamic of weirdness together in a bewildering new world, but fragile Lou was filled with rage. Maybe she was the only sane one in a crazy house. Frustrated, inarticulate, she bounced from middle-kid feuding with Joanie to middle-kid feuding with George. She went on violent rampages; most of her anger was directed at Joanie. One day she hurled a deodorant can at Joanie with such force that it flew fast and furious out the open bedroom window, leaving a crater when it smashed to earth in the baseball diamond of the Catholic school across the street. Joanie ducked, or it would surely have done her serious injury.

Lou was more than a handful: she cursed and skipped school; she bullied the twins into swiping the neighbors' milk jugs for her—in those days, a four-litre plastic milk jug was worth forty cents at the corner store. Everybody put their empties out on the doorstep for the milkman; it was easy to amass a small fortune if you were up early enough, or out late enough. Sometime over the next year, I began to get notes from Joanie, begging me to protect her from Lou. Of course I couldn't—I was in school or at work, and soon I had a social life that took me out of the house regularly. Mom couldn't handle Lou; neither could Dad, apparently, because when Lou moved away from us again later that year, it was into foster care.

Things began to come apart quickly and chaotically. I can't remember a specific event that precipitated the great unravelling, or whether there even was one. I don't know if that's because I was overwhelmed by it all, too much inundated by the wave of events to have enough perspective for an accurate chronology, or whether subsequent years of escaping into a cloud of pot smoke have impaired my memory. Maybe both: it was a dark and snarled time. Maybe I've told myself—and the world—lies for so long that telling the truth will require something like divine investigative journalism.

Now that I'm a mother, and far enough from the past that it's safe to look back, it occurs to me that the decision to have Lou placed in foster care may have been the weight under which Mom finally stumbled and fell. She didn't say so: in life many things are never said that should be, and many things are said that should have remained unsaid. 'Words can kill or heal'. That's right out of the bible: Proverbs, a source of wonderfully succinct truths.

As a young child, Lou seemed fated to bear the blight of always being misunderstood. I remember the two of us playing outside early one summer day, me five or six, Lou three or four. I was her horse as we galloped around the yard. "Giddyup, horsey!" she'd yell, and once, when the horsey was tired, "Giddyup, stupid horse!" Mom boiled out of the house like a swarm of hornets, descended on bewildered Lou, *"What did you say?!"* "Horsey, horsey!" we insisted, "Stupid horse!" but she spanked Lou anyhow.

Forever that incident niggled at my understanding: my kid self believed Mom was punishing Lou for calling me 'stupid' in our game, and 'stupid' wasn't a word that got much notice in our house. But of course what Mom heard through the open window was a word that sounded a lot like 'horse'—a word that was one of Dad's favorite invectives. How helpless she must have felt to have heard those words coming out of her baby daughter's mouth. Poor Mom: their partnership was only a handful of years old, and already the paint was coming off.

"Crosspatch" was Mom's nickname for Lou as a toddler—for a while I thought it had something to do with the patch she sometimes wore to correct a lazy eye. And I remember Mom reading us a story about a cranky lion-cub—his name was Crosspatch, and he fought with all the other animals. Lou was Mom's Crosspatch, but she was my childhood-companion sister. George and Joanie and I grew close later, but it was Lou whose memories are closest to my own, the only one who can go back nearly as far. I wonder if she remembers the day Mom called us indoors for lunch—which we called dinner—and Lou's plate held a heaping feast of sticks and stones, grass and yellow dandelion heads. For a while, everything Lou picked up from the yard got eaten; Mom must've been terrified she'd be poisoned. That was an inspired bit of parenting; Mom allowed Lou to howl at the dish of lawn trimmings for several minutes before she relented.

Lou was cured by that object lesson; if only I'd been as teachable.

I was the easy kid who learned at a young age to keep her mouth shut and her true thoughts to herself. By my mid-teens, I knew that if I was careful and quiet enough I could get away with most anything, that duping Mom was easy—she was busy with her own stuff, happy to believe whatever smooth story I presented, relieved to buy whatever showed on the surface. I found that I could garner points by being helpful. 'Points', in my egocentric economy, meant admiration: praise from grandparents and aunts and uncles who watched me step up to help my mother. It was easy; I'd always been the helpful kid, and it was a good way to be near Mom.

Lou's move into foster care didn't affect me much at the time; if anything it made my life easier. There was finally some peace in our house. But decades later—with my own loved and difficult child—I find old grief for Lou, the girl whose needs were too big for either Mom or Dad. I find old anger for my parents—especially Mom—how do you oust your wounded child from the nest? When it endangers its siblings with its thrashing about, don't you just try harder to heal its hurts? Don't you gather, stand and bind with love, then fight together for the miracle which must come, *will* come? But she didn't believe, then, in leaning, and she didn't know about miracles that come in peaceful truth, with neither sparkles nor suicidal despair. She thought leaning just meant you were weak. It *does* mean that, of course: but what Mom didn't know back then is that everybody else is weak, too—and that the only hope of finding strength is in leaning against somebody strong.

It was easy to slide along the path of least resistance, and still get what I wanted the year I turned seventeen. Not that I wanted anything in particular: I'd learned not to want or expect very much from real life. I learned nothing from the reaping and sowing that went on all around me—on my street of ne'er-do-wells, dreamers, and drunks, and just half a neighborhood away, among the homes of the successful: those who'd stayed married, gone to school, gotten the breaks. Those were the 'normal' families, of which I dared not even dream to be a member.

CHAPTER 16

But I was a kid who knew it all.

I'd been politely let go from my job at the ice-cream store: I'd glazed over too many times while my boss explained the intricacies of the old-fashioned cash register; as a result, I failed to charge my customers the appropriate taxes, and the store lost money every time I worked. Mom got me a job short-order cooking at the restaurant where she worked: only weekends at first, but gradually my hours increased. The owner was adamant, at first, that I not allow my job to interfere with school. He was divorced; his daughters were just a few years older than me. Hiring me was his way of offering Mom a helping hand—he had a crush on her, but of course Mom's faithfulness to Neil Diamond made her as serious and unavailable as a nun.

How easily I was satisfied! Every payday I proudly handed half my cheque to Mom, knowing that my contribution to our poor household really made a difference. With the other half, I was a kid in a candy store. I disposed of my income handily and happily, with the witless imprudence of a child. I *was* still a child, a sheep in wolf's clothing.

New money meant new clothes, clothes that didn't come with the musty smell of second-hand store all over them. As a youngster, one of my greatest fears was that some kid would recognize her cast-offs, and spread the word that Rainie's clothes came from the Salvation Army Thrift Store.

New clothes meant new pursuits: I discovered movies at a downtown theatre, and found to my surprise that I was finally able to follow a plot. The TV was rarely turned on when we lived at the farmhouse, and when it was, I didn't watch it—there was too much other stuff to do. As a young child I had great difficulty understanding movies—old black-and-white films on an old black-and-white TV meant that the villains and heroes all looked alike. They were all tough: they talked tough, they all smoked, and they all wore sinister-looking hats.

Only Tarzan movies and westerns were simple enough for me to follow—you always knew that in a Tarzan movie, the bad guys were the half-naked natives carrying spears, and the good guys were the terrified khaki-dressed missionaries, relying on Tarzan for their last-minute rescue from a giant cauldron. And westerns, or cowboys-and-Indians as we called them, were easy to follow, too—the white bad guys always looked sneaky or stupid, and wore black hats; and it was a safe bet that most of the 'Indians' would be bad guys, especially if there were covered wagons in the story. Outside of those reliable genres, I preferred cartoons: the plots were simple, and the faces all recognizable. Even with black-and-white cartoons, there was never any danger of confusing Bluto with Popeye.

Discovering movies at sixteen was bemusing, almost as revelatory as learning to read had been at six. It occurred to me, dimly, that my years of social maladjustment might be somehow related to my stunted ability to comprehend the stories behind all of those grey and grainy faces. What if I'd been misunderstanding the plot, and misreading the characters and scripts in real life, for years? For all of my childhood? Well then, could I ever trust my own perceptions about people?

My newfound wealth took me into greasy spoons where my friend and I could spend three dollars apiece, and sit for hours drinking coffee and dreaming aloud our deluded teen-outcast dreams. Soon we discovered bars where the staff didn't look too closely at the IDs of the high-school kids that crowded in on a Friday or Saturday night.

I was a dim-witted sheep, and Mom wasn't a very good shepherd, wandering much too near the cliff's edge herself. She was in need of her own guardian. The two events may not be connected, but Lou went into foster care that year, and Mom fell off the cliff a little while later.

One day I came home from school, and when I opened the door, there she sat on the bottom stair, huddled in a ball, rocking and moaning "I can't... I can't...." over and over again. Behind her eyes I could see the Hell she was in: they were blank and hopeless. She had gone inward and found a great, fearsome void. She remained inward and terrified, disabled to varying degrees for the next several years. Inevitably, down had followed up, and down made up pay dearly. In the words of a particularly apt Neil Diamond song, 'the higher the top, the longer the drop'; it was a long way down for all of us.

Where were the twins? They'd have been arriving home about the same time, but I don't remember them being there. Maybe I was just home for lunch; maybe Mom had called me from school.

She went to the hospital, and was admitted to the psychiatric ward, but I don't remember her getting there. Maybe she took herself; maybe she called Grandma or an aunt or uncle... Wasn't I sixteen, about to become a high school dropout working full time? When I look back, it's hazy. Wasn't it grade eleven that I joined the Outer's Club and saved almost enough money to go on the Grand Canyon white water rafting trip? Wasn't that when Mom went into the hospital? I remember the secret feeling of relief—because it was looking like I might not manage to raise the money before deadline, and using Mom's 'nervous breakdown' as my excuse was easier for me than admitting we were so poor. I was very young and selfish.

So many things happened all at once: I'd joined Junior Achievement and co-starred in a theatrical production that got my friend and me into the local newspaper. That brief acting stint funnelled me into a crowd that was so much more sophisticated than I that perhaps I was as exotic to them as they were to me. They were university students, and our little Junior Achievement theatre company was their practicum. Our director and his wife, in their early-twenties, took us with them to the university pub; there were parties in their bohemian apartment where we sat in a circle of sophistication and joie-de-vivre that was three quarters pot smoke and one quarter cheap red wine. How wonderful to be part of something big again!

When Mom went into the hospital, the stage was set for me to take over at home, which I did with diva-like self-importance. There was never open blame against her for her illness: that wouldn't have been noble or gracious, and I wanted to be noble, though I had no interest in developing any ennobling character traits, nor any deliberate guidance. Not that I'd have paid attention, necessarily—it was easy enough to blind my conscience and turn a cold back to the starving and sickened spirit within me.

The spirit-sickness that came after spending a Friday or Saturday night drinking at Rocco's Tavern was worse than any physical hangover. Somehow we'd manage to find our way back to my friend's house or to some young man's dim and dingy first apartment, where we'd sit and smoke pot, then, gluttonous from the marijuana, order a large greasy pizza and devour it like ravenous wolves. My friend and I kept an impaired eye on one another, made sure neither was lured away alone: but we drank, smoked dope, and got into any car that was on its way to a 'party'.

Surely God's grace was upon us even then; we always managed to wake up at her house the next morning, our physical virtues, at least, intact. But that next morning, for me, was always a time of loss and sadness. I felt cold and empty, far away from a good thing inside myself, and very lonely. It didn't occur to me that my debauchery might be influencing anybody else, but something inside me recognized that what I was doing was wrong.

At home it was easy to be merely dutiful. There was so much *stuff* – the twins were still in elementary school—there was supper to cook, the kitchen to clean, homework to supervise, and school lunches to be made. There was bedtime for the twins, and there was my job, too, which I'd managed to make nearly full time after agreeing to work into the small hours. Nodding off in the morning led easily to skipping classes, and skipping classes progressed naturally to dropping out entirely.

All I ever really wanted was a place where I could feel secure: school could not offer that, neither could home. Work didn't provide it either, but at least there was money. And money could buy distraction, escape. The smallest seed of self-respect, flowering to hope and perhaps even ambition, might have changed the course of my life immeasurably then. But Mom wasn't able to impart those things, if she even had them to give, and perhaps I wasn't ready to receive them.

CHAPTER 17

What I really can't believe is how *mad* I still am at her sometimes. Mad for so many reasons: she's not around to be an amazing grandma like her own mother was—another gift that was stolen. What are you supposed to give your kids? (Everything: you're supposed to give them your life.) You're supposed to be grandma, when the time comes, spoil your children's children with treats, have them for sleepovers, make them clothes and cakes, take them camping and berry-picking, take them on picnics, fold them into your plump and loving self. You are supposed to become that comfortable windfall—sweet, slightly wrinkled, but sound and full of goodness. You are supposed to embody content, to be the blessings that come with time and perseverance: wise, patient, kind, cheerful, strong.

For your children and grandchildren you are supposed to quit smoking, teach them to respect themselves, honor the bodies they've been given. You're supposed to tell them the truth: that they aren't their own, they don't belong to themselves, they weren't meant for independence or autonomy. You're supposed to teach them the reason they weren't born walking—that they're hardwired to rely on others, on parents and brothers and sisters, on friends, and above all, on God.

You are supposed to grow soft only when you're old—when you're young you need to be stronger, you have to be hard sometimes, protect your children from their own foolish selves. Mom was never hard enough for us: she set no limits. Freedom was her mantra and she thought the best way to give her kids the gift of freedom was to raise them without fences.

But she didn't know how green and foolish I was. She didn't listen, and after a while I didn't tell. (But I tried to, a long time before: the kid that I was came home from school and told her about Bucky Beaver and Fleabag and other mean words, about viciously hurled stones and spit.) She couldn't listen until years later. By then it was too late; I was lost, and whatever heartache I tried to take to her just got stuck behind all the unanswered pain of childhood.

There was a time in my early twenties she ministered to me, stroking my hair as I lay with my head in her lap, trying to weep. So many things were sad: my failed marriage; our lives—mine and my siblings', dear Mom's—so mockingly, hurtfully far from the glory I'd always imagined for us. All four of us children used drugs. We practiced serial monogamy—sometimes married, sometimes co-habiting, but never fully committed, never faithful. We were all intelligent, all had good gifts—and every one of us was a high-school dropout. Every promise of youth was stolen or squandered, and I felt my heart broken—but I could not let myself melt into my mother. If tears came, they only lasted a minute or two, and then something rose up inside me like cold steel, something in my core that turned tears to dry sand. There had been too much practice at ignoring hurt, too many comfortless years of knowing that crying means you are to be despised: a skinny, pale, and spineless nothing whose bladder is too close to its eyes. Crying was worse than useless—it didn't bring emotional relief, it didn't solve any problems, it hurt my chest and throat, swelled my eyes, and made my face blotchy. Moms compassion was there for me, but years of being her confidante had warped our mother-daughter relationship, reversed our roles. I didn't know how to be comforted by her compassion.

But I loved her for trying, anyway.

The summer I turned fifteen, our last summer at the farmhouse, had also been the final summer of my childhood. Mom didn't know what a clumsy, frightened thing I was inside my new body; it didn't occur to me to tell her. June, my grade nine year, I left school a kid, and in September I returned a young woman, so physically changed that one of my friends remarked how dramatically I'd bloomed over the summer. In two short months I'd developed breasts, gotten my period, and shot up a couple of inches. But inside, I was still the same shy loner, safer and happier in the woods than anywhere else.

Mom didn't tell me how to live in my new body. She didn't tell me that people—boys—would begin to treat me differently. She'd given me the little pink book—I came home from school in grade five and found it on my pillow, read through it, asked about tampons, and felt feminine and mysterious for a few days. She answered all of my questions. Privy to those secrets of womanhood, I was honored when she sent me to Merrick's store for the big box of pads which in those days were kept discreetly hidden behind the door.

But the wonderful promise of womanly transformation faded to the distant background when my body showed no signs of changing within a few months. Of course I was a late bloomer: I'd been a late walker, maybe a late talker, and I was socially awkward and immature in every other way; and though I was full of beautiful words, they too were latent and hidden. At 15, I was the butterfly that didn't realize its caterpillar days were over;

I kept a caterpillar soul for some time. But others saw my new body. Boys noticed me.

How embarrassing to wake up in the night decades later, feeling mad enough at Mom that it's impossible to get back to sound and peaceful sleep. How ridiculous to be angry now: but maybe I'd been angry for years and years. That's probably what a psychologist would say—I compartmentalized all of my old anger, shoved it away and hidden it so I could avoid dealing with it. I still fight it—still say to myself things like—well, it was a different world back in those days, parents lived in a separate universe, people didn't really know what was going on inside their kids and the kids, for the most part, were just fine with that. The generation gap was a real thing back then. My siblings and I lived imaginary lives of which our parents had no notion—we were explorers, we were talking animals, an alligator lived under our beds. Parents weren't quite as in touch with the minutiae of their kids' lives as they are now.

I say to myself—she was sick, she had a mental illness that made it impossible for her to pay attention to anybody other than herself. (Isn't that simply selfishness?) Oh, those are hard, cold words! But she wasn't a hard, cold person—she was warm and generous and funny and creative and wonderful—and the world revolved around her. I was happy to be a satellite; it gave me a purpose, at least for a while.

Her parenting was always more about her than us; she was our friend, she was the cool mom, cooler than everybody else's parents. Our friends adored her; many of the neighborhood kids called her 'Mom'. Even her handwriting had a fan club—my grade ten math teacher traded notes with her on the backs of my weekly quizzes: her graceful cursive caught his attention first, but soon he was drawn in by her witty parental commentary.

Only now do I see how self-centred my memory has been—because of course she loved us fully and unconditionally, and it is the lens of my own egotistical perception that shows me a woman whose 'parenting was always more about her than us'. Only now do I recognize my envy of her sparkle—forever I believed that I wasn't jealous. My siblings and I were proud of our mother the star. She was fun. It is only as an adult that I see her faults, and resent the glamour and self-centredness that stole her away from us. I wonder which deadly character flaw of my own will warp my children... But my kids and I have the advantage of truth and grace, advantages my mother didn't have. We know already that we are fallen and imperfect. We keep one another on the right path, forgive one another and provide correction when we stray.

But my mother was on a dogmatic quest for freedom, and every piece of motherly advice came through that filter. Once, seventeen and still relatively untouched by the world—certainly untouched by boys—I wandered around Lakeside Park enjoying the sunshine. I'd have been dressed for the scorching Ontario summer in short cut-off jeans and a halter top, barefoot, no doubt, and carrying a sketch pad or notebook. That was me expressing my artistic freedom and selfhood, cheered on by Mom who was probably vicariously re-doing her own straitened teen years.

But I was really just a child playing with a loaded gun.

Approached by a suave and sophisticated sailor, a man in his thirties with a sailboat berthed at the Port Dalhousie Marina, I was immensely flattered by his attention. There was another girl on his boat, about my own age; the three of us shared a bottle of wine. He was from Toronto, and also kept an apartment in St. Catharines. He seemed a perfect gentleman, and invited me to meet him again the next afternoon. I rode the bus home and told Mom all about him, leaving out the bottle of wine. Mom's experience with Dad's drinking had left an indelible mark: there was never alcohol in our house. It would be another ten years before she'd allow herself to enjoy a cold bottle of beer after mowing the lawn on a hot day.

Her response, when I told her about my sailor 'friend', astonished me even then, and saddens me now that I have a daughter of my own. "It may be the best thing that ever happens to you," was what she said. She didn't ground me, or even question my judgement; she said nothing about his being twice my age—had not a word of caution for me. There was no motherly digging for further information: if she sensed there was more to the story than I was telling, she didn't say so.

Perhaps I misunderstood her. Maybe I misread her as completely as she misheard Lou that long-ago summer morning. Did she envision a long and happy liaison for me, with a twenty-years-older spouse, a marriage as successful as the one enjoyed by her aunt and uncle? I'd expressed my desire for a big brother many times; did she hope I'd found that protector-lover? Maybe she imagined a better life for me, a glamorous life of plenty, with this man who owned a boat, and had apartments in two cities... Maybe she really had no idea that inside my new body I was still very much a child.

It was Lou who warned me to steer clear of him. Though she was younger, she was much more worldly than I; Lou got all the edited-out details when I shared the story with her on a weekend visit. Lou knew about the bottle of wine, heard that this smooth older man had offered to take me to live in his apartment across the Lake in Toronto, and promised to make me 'the most sensuous woman in the world.' To be fair, had I been as forthright with Mom, her motherly instincts might have kicked in. Lou bluntly informed me that he was a pimp, and then explained what a pimp was, as I had no idea.

Mom just didn't know how truly foolish I was. I knew her a lot better than she knew me: she made sure people knew who she was, but my reserve kept most everyone out. (Couldn't she have *listened*, once, seen that her idiot-child daughter was heading into danger? She should have warned me about sharks and wolves, that there are predators who slaver over witless lambs, eat them up and discard the empty carcass with less thought than they might give to scratching an itch.) How could she have been so blind, so *thoughtless*? Or was she as truly naive as I, clinging in spite of the evidence to a candy-coated notion that we all have one another's best interests at heart, generally, and that everything will work out okay in the end...

CHAPTER 18

Isn't it funny how everything did work out in the end...?
The other day I found some old letters she'd written me, after I drifted out here, letters that reminded me how guileless she was, how, though lost, full of love. And love, of course, covers over a multitude of sins. Even mine.

For one thing, I ran away, over and over again.

At eighteen I ran. "There is nothing else here for me," I said to Mom heartlessly, words as hard and cold as ball bearings. I moved out, left Mom and George and Joanie to look after each other without me. Who knew where Lou was? She was everywhere and nowhere; I worked and smoked pot sometimes, and hardly thought about my tormented sister. Mom was mostly out of the hospital by then, and generally functioning on a regimen of antidepressants and lithium. She worked, off and on, and I assuaged my guilt by giving her money on a semi-regular basis.

I moved out and enjoyed playing house. I was a high-school drop-out, but I had a full-time job and an apartment. I paid my bills on time and bought new clothes. I gave Mom money, and still had enough left over to buy marijuana. For two years I worked and partied, never looking ahead for consequences, or back for insight.

I ran, I thought, toward 'normal'; other girls my age partied, had boyfriends and sex. That's what I wanted, too—just to be 'normal'. So I got myself a boyfriend, gave myself away, had him move in with me. Mom didn't like him. Neither did I, really, but there was little understanding of my own motives, and even less self-respect. The need to fit in, to believe that my life was normal, was my primary drive; if I could just attain 'normal', that would be more than enough for me.

At twenty I ran. I ran from the boyfriend I didn't like, and who didn't particularly like me. I got married hoping that a 'successful' marriage would give my life some meaning. My handsome husband had an engineering degree and a guitar; and he came from a hard-working eastern European immigrant family, the kind of family that sticks together, no matter what. Though I was hugely relieved when my own parents split up, I was drawn like a magnet to strong marriages. Joe's parents were still married, a huge plus in my books. He didn't drink too much, and only smoked dope once in a while. He was, for the most part, a decent young man. Surely, then, with his normal background, Joe must have whatever it takes to be 'normal'. Maybe, by association and osmosis, my own life would begin to take a 'normal' course...

I was married like a doll is married—I played house again, glibly, without any notion of the magnitude of solemn commitment that ought to go into a lifelong partnership. My marriage to Joe was as flimsy as my parents' had been, and for many of the same reasons; we barely knew each other, and I, at least, barely knew myself. We shared no common foundation, certainly nothing deep or strong enough to support a lasting union. Immature as I was, it wasn't long before we separated.

Apparently I'd been seeking the wrong thing—'normal' wasn't to be for me after all; how could it be, coming from where I did? I needed to be true to... something different, maybe... So I worked and lived alone again for a while, and practiced being free.

Free to party, free to squander myself. Free to focus entirely upon myself—but what happens when you find out you're hollow? You can collapse in on yourself, like Mom did—an honest response, but one I was too proud to allow myself. Or you can try to fill that space.

There must be *somebody* for me: somebody who fits me, who'll make me feel safe, somebody who'll make me the centre of his universe.

So I found someone else to pin my hope and need on, and Joe died young a few years later, of complications from juvenile diabetes.

At just twenty-seven, I was a separated widow living common-law with an unfaithful lout.

I was head-over-heels: he was a sweet-faced dope-smoking country boy, one of a brood of twelve. His unpretentious upbringing and blue collar parents appealed to my unearned and secret snobbery. Though intelligent, he was barely literate; and I was seven years older, which in his eyes endued me with endless mystique. Around Mel and his family it was easy to be smart and sophisticated. His parents were still married, too, and they adopted me as carelessly as they might take in a stray cat. After twelve children, what's another daughter, more or less?

I ran away from him, too, outraged by his eventual infidelity, blind to my own. I ran from him to yet another would-be rescuer. And this one I married; only to discover that he was a runaway, too, fleeing a chaotic upbringing at the hands of a mentally ill parent.

Together we ran away to the west coast.

Of course, it didn't look like running away at the time. It looked like adventure, like running *to*. Running to a fresh start, where nobody knew me or my woman-at-the-well past, where there were neither lies nor truths attached to my name.

But there is no do-it-yourself makeover—you can't re-invent yourself as long as you're covered with all the dirt of the past. No matter how competent and articulate in your new job, how well-intentioned in your new marriage, you cannot change yourself simply by changing your environment. You can't change yourself from the outside, because you can't get outside yourself, either to see properly or to do the work that needs to be done; and you can't change yourself from the inside because you are right there *with* yourself, getting in the way. It's a lost cause. You can't save yourself from the past, or from any of the shortcomings that will inevitably screw up your present and future.

But I tried, anyway: I ran away from my siblings, from Mom and Neil Diamond, from my distant and secretly despised father, from dear Grandma and Grandpa and all of the good aunts and uncles and cousins.

I ran from a train-wreck of a life: mayhem littered every side. I ran from despair, from being unable to learn from my mistakes. I ran believing I could leave it all behind, and found to my horror that it was stuck to me like a bad smell.

For a while I pretended that everything was better.

That's how it was: years ago I drifted lost and blind, a tumbleweed heading west unanchored, just another insubstantial detritus at the whim of every gust of circumstance.

And found myself, surprised, blundering against the familiar.

When you're lost you look for landmarks; to someone who's grown up in the shadow of Vesuvius, Mount St. Helen's looks a lot like home... You may recognize danger, yes, but there is the daunting, seductive comfort of its familiarity. Like an addict after her fix, or a mote of cosmic flotsam caught in the orbit of an imploding star, I was drawn, helpless, to those symptoms: huge personality, shimmering charisma. (But not entirely helpless: the truth is that there *was* an alarm—that still, small voice, heard but unheeded: "No; this is wrong." The voice that would remain ignored for years...)

It didn't matter that I was married—there's something about him, an aura of mystery and knowledge—here is a man who has glimpsed the Bigger Picture. He has seen that there is *so much more going on*; he talks about it, and it's all over him. He was brilliant and sparkling, but entirely focussed on self-illumination. (He's like Mom...)

I'm the moth who thinks the flickering porch light is God.

I'm the woman who believes *this* man can save her: save her from poverty, save her from purposelessness. So I ran again. I left my second husband; callous of the impact on him, and with hardly a cursory nod to caution or decency, I attached myself like a hopeful burr to this new promise.

Ten years later we had two boys, still youngsters, and a baby girl not yet walking—and maybe I was pregnant again. And he, sporadically employed, his emotions suddenly spiralling out of control, caricature-huge: "Get an abortion," he urged.

CHAPTER 19

I took the kids to meet the rest of their family this past summer. Something happened there, but I'm not yet sure just what it was... I thought I went prepared for the worst, because after all, we've been apart for over twenty years, my siblings and I. I went trying hard not to hope for the best. Carefully I reasoned against blood covenant recognized, of healing reunion.

Good thing, because they were all in hiding.

As for me, I have fallen back into an old trap: the heartache of separation from my wandering brother and sisters instead deferred to the beautiful land left behind. Peace outside the school-bus window, but never in my heart; grief for the green hills of home-far-away stands for the unshed tears for those lost and orphaned children. (Keep your heart safe behind that strong, cold glass...) And I miss the good aunts and uncles and cousins who stood in the gap, faithful memory-bearers, for absent Lou and George and Joanie. Homesick, now, for a lovely boreal island where dear people shared new old times...

But I'm hurt *they* didn't want to see me, didn't care to know niece and nephews. Are they mad at me for running away, mad I wasn't there for Mom? Is it just easier to say, "Well, she's been gone so long; she wasn't around to be an aunt to *our* children; why should we care?" Why should they? (But I wanted to see them, see how they've grown, coped or not, tell them I'm sorry I wasn't a better sister. I wanted to know how—whether—they managed to deal with the whole Neil Diamond thing.)

I don't even know what I'm supposed to tell next.

Again I couldn't save my brother and sisters, any more than when I was ten years old with dreams of running away through the snowy night woods to a better life. I'm as powerless now as I was then. What am I supposed to do with the heartache? Let it fester? Pretend it isn't there, ignore it and hope it finally just goes away? Live with it, all the while knowing it doesn't even work as inoculation against future loss and separation...?

That's a bitter pill. I can't accept that. If I do, then I must accept the loss of my own children to a blank and pointless end. If I do, I cannot count myself as one of *His* children, because *He* loves *all* of us, and wants all of us safely home. (Am I okay with any of *my* children wandering lost? If one child puts himself in the way of danger, even if he endangers the rest of us, am I okay with letting him blunder without intervention, headlong off the cliff?)

Never.

Mom told me many years ago of a vision she once had. Going back with eyes wide open, perhaps I can hope to discern, however 'through a glass darkly', the difference between her psychosis and, perhaps, a God-given vision.

So her vision of the five of us safely on the mountain-top might have been one of God's gifts to her, a truly precious jewel she picked up along with the shiny rubbish, and passed down to me all unknowing.

Isn't it interesting that I'm the only one who lives anywhere near an actual mountaintop – and though I was running away, I finally got here by following the signs that sent me back into the past... Isn't that divine synchronicity? That is the work of an Author, who wrote every sign for me, the daughter whose life has always been lived between the lines, somewhere between the literal and the figurative.

This all began as a quest to finally put Mom's illness in its place – somewhere far, far behind me. I hoped I could do that without ever acknowledging the price we paid, my siblings and I, in pain and loss. Separate Mom from her illness, and you've separated yourself from resenting her; it's ok to hate a disease. And once you've separated yourself from resentment, you're free from any obligation to seek forgiveness for it. You're free from any duty to forgive her for her part in it, too.

Too bad it isn't that easy.

I couldn't separate Mom from her delusion, after all. It was part of her, and there is only one Physician great enough to excise the lies from her psyche. But something *did* happen while I was walking around in those long ago days and years...

When I think of her now, it isn't primarily resentment that I feel; it's a bemusing mix of affection, admiration and exasperation. I can't wait to hug her and kiss her again, and tell her thank you. After all, didn't she live the most amazing example of fidelity, of integrity that went far beyond the practical? It was Mom who encouraged my own unarticulated quest for truth and beauty. It is true that she could not provide the direction and discipline I needed, but it is also true that she lived a shining example of love and grace.

And I feel just a hint of pity, too, because there's still that question, perhaps not to be resolved this side of Heaven—did she or did she not *choose* to live in a lie? (Was it, entirely, a lie?)

Maybe it doesn't even matter: maybe the point is that it isn't for me to judge, just to be thankful for the gifts she gave, and to forgive the rest. She lived her fragile life epically; a grace-note, perhaps intended to distract us from the successful pursuit of worldly gain. How can you come from a mother who's shown you these things, and then grow up to be satisfied with anything like normal?

I must believe she finally found the only true love that satisfies the heart-hunger we are all born with. And I must never stop believing that Lou and George and Joanie are on their way up the mountain.

"I am writing your story," that's what He said. Well. My story is this: here I am. I have joy. I have roots and a family. My children are nourished; they are not abandoned, not Fatherless. There is peace, even in the lonely times, even when life looks chaotic. How did that happen, after a beginning that must lead inevitably to disaster and cold, empty death?

How do you make that story what it is? (You don't; *He* does.)

CHAPTER 20

For no reasonable reason, I can't agree to an abortion. Dread is the only constant in my life: the fear that there might soon be another child to feed and care for is just more of the same. Everyday there is walking-on-eggshells as I try not to set him off on a tangential three-hour rant; every month there's the anxiety of having to tell the landlord, again, that there can only be partial payment of the rent. There is dread of a failure too profound and shameful to face: that the only life I can provide my children is the one that I had, the one I swore to myself they would not have to live. The dread of raising them to accept poverty and insecurity, dreary prospects and meanness; the shame of condemning them to patched and brow-beaten mediocrity without hope of standing up to try on nobility. But: *I know there must be more.* That truth is entrenched deep in my guts. I've always known, since childhood... There *is* more: but I don't have it; and if I don't have it, how can I give it to them?

You cannot say to your little boys, "Don't dare to dream, because I can't give you *anything*—it turns out I haven't got anything of value to give. No roots, no family, no protection, no wisdom; nothing." Who can say those things—who can even think them? There's terrible irony to my life: I want so badly to have a partnership, a marriage that lasts, but we aren't even married. I want to give my children a strong and safe home and family, because I didn't have one myself. I want so badly not to fail at this that I stay in it long after I know it's doomed, long past the point where it's healthy for any of us. And instead of nothing, I offer my children diversions: there are plenty of those, enough for everybody, lots of shiny stuff lying on the side of the road—just like Mom.

I taught them some good things: how to read, early—they were so bright and eager they lapped it up like hungry puppies; the names of neighborhood flowers, how to recognize the chives, mint, rosemary, and catnip growing behind our apartment building.

Carless, I took them on long, long walks: we walked everywhere, my young children and I. Walk to the park, walk home. Walk down to the river, watch tugboats, play in the water, fly a kite, walk back home again—a mile-and-a-half each way. Look at the budding new shoots in spring; see the anthills, and last year's ragged oriole's nest still hanging from an apple-tree branch like a holey old sock... We look at bugs, at all manner of small and crawling creatures. I teach them my old habit: rescue the poor city-dwelling earthworm, stranded on a sunny sidewalk after the rain. Get him into the grass or under a leaf quick, before he's fried as crisp as a dry chow mien noodle.

They learn to enjoy weather: be glad when the sun shines, splash in the omnipresent west-coast puddles, sniff out the salt-and-juniper spice of sea and mountain on the wind. We don't have pets, but they learn to be kind and gentle with the neighbor's cat when it drops in uninvited from time to time.

I do my best, and they grow; they don't know they are poor.

Some of these shining diversions are true treasures: I try to teach them to be thankful, to allow joy in, to love one another, to revere life; but why?

We are nearly six months behind on our rent. If our long-suffering landlord finally decides to evict us, will it matter that my children are polite and respectful? Am I setting them up only to be crushed by disappointment? What will they gain from learning to recognize beauty where it grows in the cracks of the sidewalk? Somehow, I know these things are pointless in and of themselves—only distractions to keep the children from realizing my hands are truly empty.

If they had no hope for a future—and they didn't—why should it matter whether they learned the Golden Rule, or right from wrong? If there was no hope of giving them something better, *anything* better, why couldn't I agree to smother the seed that might be germinating within me? Certainly that would've been the most practical course; it has become apparent their father cannot provide for them, either. He's as poor and tattered, as ignorant, as I: but he's shiny, he has music.

That's what he gives them: music, beautiful music, while I work. Bewildered, I go back to work because he doesn't, and nobody can eat music. I don't see that he is—flawed, faulty: he can't see ahead, he sees only the moment he's in, and he looks only at himself. He's lost in a hall of mirrors. (And me, all I see is ahead: I'm so focussed on looking ahead and seeing disaster, I stop functioning in the present. Like the deer caught in the headlights, I'm so immobilized by imminent doom that I can't take a single step to save us.) It didn't matter so much before the babies came—he usually worked, too, in those days. We lived comfortably enough until I got pregnant. Then, just days before our first child was born, he quit his job. "I want to be with you," he said. I didn't wonder very often what would happen after our baby came, how the rent and bills would be paid while both of us stayed home with a newborn. Wondering about those things frightened me deeply.

Our first son was born, and his father worked on-again off-again. I smiled, basked in the joy of new motherhood, and resolutely pushed my worry down. Our second son was born only twenty months later, and while we scrabbled to survive, I found a blessing. I had feared, during the second pregnancy, that I could never love another human being as deeply and completely as I loved my dear firstborn. Then our second son came, and he brought a gift along with him: I discovered to my joy that love is not a reasonable equation. Love somehow multiplied—without any effort on my part I had enough for both boys. My second-born son was as precious to me as life itself, as precious as his brother. I loved them individually and separately, and I loved them together. They were my two dear boys, and when I thought about what I'd do for them—well, what *wouldn't* I do for them?

They grew, and I worked, while their father was hired and fired from a score of jobs. It was always a variation on the same theme: they didn't appreciate him, the new boss was a dictatorial tyrant; one company even had ties to organized crime. The stories always came with just enough credibility to lull my doubt into uneasy suspension—they were stories told by a man at the mercy of a faulty brain chemistry, to a woman who needed above all else to believe in *something bigger*. It was Mom and Neil Diamond again, only this time it was the father of my children, and instead of a psychic lover there was an invisible force bent on keeping him down.

But my boys were *little* boys: they had to eat. We needed to keep the hydro on; I had to give *something* to the landlord. And the head of the house was lost in dreams and delusion.

So I was at work by six every morning, home by mid-afternoon to be Mom to my good boys; and while I slogged my day away in black resentment, our daytime apartment was a place of wit and charisma, pipe-dreams and poetry. Days that their lost father should have been working, or looking for work, were spent at the piano, or in grandiose salons around our kitchen table with easily charmed fringe-dwelling neighbors. They'd sit and make music, drink coffee and smoke cigarettes, talk endlessly about important movies and the dark brilliance of Nietzsche while I worked and my little boys ate Kraft Dinner and went about with un-brushed teeth and soiled clothing.

Bitterly, I realized I'd been duped by an old enemy: that demon bi-polar disorder. I should have hated it and feared it; instead, I came to hate and fear its host.

And finally there we all were: my dear girl was a baby, my girl whose conception was not celebrated the way her brothers' had been. Because nothing had changed; the pattern of lost jobs was frighteningly more than an immature rut. Every 'temporary setback' was met with greater scepticism. We lived hand-to-mouth, and our children became pawns, hostages for the generosity of disappointed family. Only constant 'borrowing', and our landlord's sorely-tested compassion, came between us and the street.

Things were at last coming to their inevitable crisis; no amount of skilful juggling could keep the hard truth of our situation from crashing down on me.

It was around this time that I began to attend church. At first it was sporadic, just to be polite to the sister-in-law whose sparkle was something like her brother's. (But she talked incessantly, embarrassingly, about Jesus, about how He'd changed her life. I liked her, but there was this awkward *obsession* of hers...) Then I went because I had nothing better to do, after all, on a Sunday, and because going to church gave me a few hours outside of the prison my home had become. By the time our daughter was a few months old I was going more or less regularly, glad of the opportunity to introduce my kids to something I'd never had: roots in a bigger community, a chance to build relationships that might last a long time, maybe a lifetime...

How I envied the people I saw there—people who'd grown up together in the same neighborhoods, known one another since high-school, or even kindergarten, some of them. (Maybe if my children belong to something as respectable and comfortably middle-class as church—if I make sure they're surrounded by socially successful and stable people, they won't be doomed to failure.)

I went to church for many reasons; I didn't go for *the* reason. I did not acknowledge that He called me. (If I admit to myself that He called me, I have to also admit I've been listening to the wrong voices for decades. If I believe He called me, then maybe *I'm* crazy... If I say out loud, "He called me," I'll have to make a commitment; maybe I'll lose the option of choosing which voice gets my attention. So I hedge my bets. I go to church, but I don't admit anything to myself, and I certainly don't say anything.)

I was the kid mad at her parent, but too hungry to run away. Instead, I sat at the dinner table, sulking and glowering.

I went to church, but I did not enjoy it.

I did not like meeting the people who seemed to get it; meeting them made me feel like an imposter. (All those warm and genuine smiles, and mine, plastered on my face as falsely as clown make-up; couldn't they tell I wasn't really one of them?) I liked listening to the sermons, as long as they focused on the human condition—that was interesting. But when the sermons moved away from the problem, and looked instead at the Solution, I was lost again. Intellectually, I understood—it made sense. It felt like a true story, that gospel. It was an equation: of course life must be paid for with death. What else? And eternal life—Life!—must be paid for with Death. I got it: my own little death could never be enough to pay for Life, because my own life had been little and tawdry and mean. But Jesus—*His* life and death *are* enough, if you accept that He Himself is God, and that He took on the Death half of the equation because He loves us, and knows we're utterly incapable. That appealed to me; it made wonderful good sense. But it wasn't *alive* in me, it wasn't *my* truth. Those church people had something else that I didn't have, and I didn't like that. It gave me that old feeling of being an outsider again, and I'd had enough of not belonging.

Most of all, I didn't like the worship.

I hated the way the music made me feel: nostalgic and weepy, like hearing my name called across fields and years, the voice of somebody who loves me calling me home for supper and bedtime... I hated my emotional response to it, so akin to my childhood response to Grandpa's fiddle: feet can't stay still, ears cannot stay deaf, and heart struggles to break free of its stony entombment. It fights hard against my will that it remain catatonic. (Nearly dead may not be fully alive, but at least it doesn't hurt, much.)

How that worship music made me squirm, embarrassed and resentful. I distrusted my response, I told myself, because I'm one of those people who respond too easily. I have a facile emotional constitution—I cry watching "Rudolph the Red Nosed Reindeer" for Heaven's sake, because it evokes childhood so poignantly. Bagpipes start instant tears. So while those Christians are worshiping, I gulp and swallow and blink; I fight so hard against weeping that I'm sweating and itchy. Every reserve of strength goes to my self-restraint: I will NOT cry, I will NOT raise my hands and wave my arms, though every cell in my body longs to join in that dance. (But I'm NOT one of them. I won't be a hypocrite!)

I distance myself, and work hard to distrust the motive behind the music. I tell myself that this is a tactic, skilled showmanship used to work the crowd into an emotional frenzy, a way to soften everybody up for the coming sermon. It doesn't occur to me that most everybody is there because they *want* to be, that they might actually be experiencing real freedom and joy. It's just music - how deeply can simple music bring you into spiritual awareness? It's too easy, too temporary; all emotion and no thought. I can't approach Christianity that way.

I don't want that great upwelling of mere emotion clouding my reason. I tell myself the emotion should be the wonderful icing on the cake, to be eaten last and savoured because it's the sweetest, the reward for having attained a mature understanding of the truth. IF—and it's a big if—I ever give up and really commit to Christ, it's going to be on *my* terms. All that embarrassing dancing and weeping among a crowd of strangers makes me squeamish. (But that worship music makes me feel like I want nothing more than to surrender. But how deep is that feeling? How permanent is that easy sweeping away? Very shallow, I think; and very temporary. I know myself. I know how easily I'm moved, how little it takes, and how hard I have to fight against strong emotion. Intense emotion makes people lose control—lose their ability to function, to raise their children. That kind of intensity lands people in psychiatric wards.)

There's a distinction between spiritual understanding and having an emotional response to the understanding. Proud and fearful, I want the understanding first, and the joy a manageable and watered-down second. I want it to be polite: tidy, and without all that unseemly involvement of the heart. After all, I'm a cerebral person; my heart may leap, yes, but my mind keeps it well away from dizzying heights. In my experience, dizzying heights come with terrifying drops. (I don't see myself, though: not really. I've forgotten my one deep childhood longing: to fly. And smart as I am, I don't see that it isn't understanding that I lack. Because how could I possibly have an emotional reaction to a spiritual truth that I don't comprehend?! I don't realize that what I'm *really* missing is a relationship with a Person.)

It stayed like that for a year or more, until that July when my girl was still an infant, and it was looking like I was pregnant again.

"'Get an abortion,'" he urged.

CHAPTER 21

That was the bitter, absolute end of my self-reliance. Here was a circumstance that could neither be sidestepped nor ignored: I was pregnant, but another baby was simply out of the question. And I would not, could not consider an abortion.

Utter defeat is a terrible thing to face. The granite fact of NO ESCAPE induces panic; like a blind rat in a maze you bump into the same walls over and over, until you're in a hopeless stupor. Can't have another baby; can't get an abortion; can't think about the mess this whole situation will cause... The apartment is already too small, he's not working most of the time, and I've finally had to resort to welfare to keep us fed. Can I even imagine explaining this to family? "I'm pregnant, but I'm going to give this baby up for adoption..." How do you tell the other children that we can't keep their new brother or sister? I couldn't even contemplate suicide: I was too responsible and too proud to consider leaving my kids alone, especially that way; and if a medically-managed abortion was unthinkable, certainly abortion by suicide could never be an option either.

More beaten-down than I'd been since childhood, and incapacitated by fear for our future, I sat in my chair that July evening, and weeping, I prayed. "I give up. Jesus, if You are real," I said, "please take over. My life is completely ruined."

A bit melodramatic, but He answered me right away.

It didn't matter that even in the darkest midst of misery, part of me felt foolish. (What if I'm talking to myself?) If He was offended by my divided mind, He let it go. He rescued me the way I rescued my children when they needed it: first things first. When my little ones fell down and skinned their knees, the first thing I did was determine where my attention was most required. If they were really bleeding, I washed and bandaged their injuries, and then I hugged and kissed and calmed them. If they were more frightened than wounded, then I held them first. And when they were ready to go out and play again, that's when I was motherly: "Next time, don't run on the sidewalk." "Don't grab stuff away from your brother, and maybe he won't slug you."

The first answer I got was deep and permanent Peace, a Peace which moved in immediately. My problems were all still there, but the insurmountable fear had fled. Secure within that deep peace, I found I had strength enough to visit my doctor, explain my dilemma, and get a pregnancy test which came back negative. There was strength to take a hard look at my life, to admit that I didn't have the resources to rear my children on my own: I was broke, materially and spiritually. It took another year, but finally there was strength to allow that I needed to get out of the orbit of their father's illness, give us all a chance to experience some of that Peace.

Anxiety didn't just pack up and leave forever: after all, I'm an uneducated single mother, raising my children in one of the most expensive cities in the world. But anxiety is never more than a temporary visitor. That Peace is so big there's no space for long-term worry. Peace, it turns out, is roomy: there's room for dealing with the stuff I have to deal with—running a house, having a job, raising my kids. And there's room for the second answer: Joy.

So many good things came back, things I hadn't even realized were missing. Yearning returned, first as melancholy. Full of self-pity, I saw how much of my life I'd squandered, and it saddened me. There was this treasure inside me now, this Person who was there for me to rely on for direction, even for a new life, but I had yet to realize the truth of that. I had the Person, but it took me a while to learn what He was there for.

The apartment was too small for me and my three little kids, but I dared not hope for anything bigger or better. "Hope deferred makes the heart sick…" That's the truth I lived in, still too young in my faith for the second half of that proverb to offer anything: "…but the dream fulfilled is a tree of life." But I turned my face away from dreams, applied my nose to the grindstone, and began to work very hard at being a Christian.

At mealtimes, I stared out my kitchen window at the neighbor's big cedar tree swaying against the sky. Resolutely I avoided daydreams, but even without a daydream to replace the tight little lane between apartment buildings, there was enough green-and-blue to give me a mini-serenity. That big old cedar—big and old by city standards—was always in my field of vision, and it was the only thing worth looking at, unless you didn't care.

Evocative, when all you can see is tree and sky: anything might be in the background—a castle maybe, or a shimmering silver-green sea of windswept ripening oats; and somehow reliable, always doing the same dance with the sky. The toss of crown and shimmy of trunk are as entertaining as they are necessary in accordance with the laws of nature, but mostly I watched the cedar just because it was there, and it looked nicer than anything else out my windows. I appreciated that all I could see from my kitchen table vantage point was the top two-thirds of my cedar. It was on a bit of a hill, and the next apartment building blocked it from the midriff down. My window was just high enough, and my chair just low enough, that I couldn't see any of the grubby alleyway. Even though I knew they were there, I couldn't see the overflowing garbage cans, the open garage, the ubiquitous blue recycling bins and ever-present McDonald's litter. Just my beautiful tree, dark green and content against the changing sky...

Fear was gone from our home, but it had yet to be replaced by hope. For some time that absence of fear was enough. My children were tidy and fed, and the cramped and dingy little apartment was clean. I ate up the Christian milieu—going faithfully to church and bible studies and prayer group meetings—without tasting much of Christ. I kept Jesus behind a door in my head – for a while He stood in Neil Diamond's spot.

Carefully, carefully I tested those waters: people *might* indeed be His body here on earth, but people, after all, are human, with the all-too-human potential to harm. I was very cautious, and for several years I lived waiting for the other shoe to drop. But nobody called me 'Fleabag', nobody told me to sit down and shut up, and nobody committed the unforgiveable sin of patronizing or condescending to me because of my poverty. Nobody hinted that I didn't belong; no-one pointed out that my financial circumstances might be greatly improved if only I quit smoking.

Time passed, and my children grew; we needed a bigger place.

Washing dishes at my kitchen sink one evening, tired of making do, tired of grey poverty, peevish with dissatisfaction, I spat like an angry cat—"I hate this rat hole!" And there came a Voice, almost audibly—"If you aren't thankful for what you have now, why should I give you more?" Why indeed? It was a question that brought me up short, made me stop what I was doing and take a good look around. We had enough to eat. I saw my healthy children; we had a roof over our heads—I saw that the apartment, though small and shabby, was clean and tidy. I'd managed to finally get the rent caught up. I was enrolled in a course at a local college that would improve my options for employment. My little daughter went to a Christian daycare; my two boys were doing well at school. Our church was several miles away, and we had no car, but dear people made sure my three kids and I got a ride back and forth almost every week. There was tremendous blessing in my life, and I wasn't acknowledging any of it.

My eyes were opened, and soon I was seeing grace and kindness and plenty everywhere. I began to practice noticing the wealth around me, and thanking God conscientiously for every good thing in my life. Soon it became apparent that He knew I meant it, because one day a promise whispered in: "I'm giving you a car, a house, a cat, and a job." Just like that. Did I want those things? Of course I did; did I ask for them? No. That's the kindness and grace of God the Father—He gives good things even to the children who don't yet know enough to ask for them. I love Him because He loved us, first.

I told my kids: God is going to give us a house, a car, a cat, and a job.

Normally in this world, the job comes first, and everything else follows because you've earned it. But God does things His own way, perhaps so there can be no doubt that it's His hand orchestrating things. So the house came first.

Not just any house, either. God who made me knows me: He could have simply given us a bigger apartment, but He gave us instead a quirky old house with creaky hardwood floors and a huge fireplace, steep wooden stairs, and bedrooms where the ceilings slope under the roof. *Our* house: some people don't care about houses, and that's fine—that's how He put them together. But I care about houses. I look at the outside of a house and get a kind of mental snapshot of the lives that have been lived there. Houses are like the people who've lived in them: they can be sad or joyful, reserved or open. My house looked a bit lonely, but welcoming: like it needed a family in it again.

We moved, and then came a job, and a cat, followed by a car, and finally an even better job. I asked for the first job; Simon the kitten was adopted for twelve dollars from a friend who was even needier than I. Everything else was a straight-out gift.

In the last few years, my personal blessings have piled up beyond belief. When I look around my home I'm astonished by the generosity of God's people, who have indeed turned out to be merely human, just as I suspected they might. Except I've changed: when people hurt me—which still does happen occasionally—I find myself forgiving them. And they're obliged to forgive me, too, when I screw up, which makes for strong and genuine friendships.

So many riches have come my way: appliances, furniture, food and clothing, a car, a van, money, more money, even more money, work, and a trip across the country to see dear Mom before she died. My kids have been treated by people who know they don't get fun trips with grandparents, and I've been blessed by people who know I don't get out much because I'm a single mother, and there just isn't money for things like a night at the opera, or weekends at a women's retreat.

I'm living proof that God's people love and nurture the widows and orphans. My house grows daily in prosperity and influence. The bounty that has come my way—both spiritual and material—doesn't diminish. I have enough—I have more than enough; I have so much that I can freely give, too, and yet the more I give away, the more He provides.

He's given me friends and neighbors who love me in spite of my reserve, with a true-hearted love that, on its way to becoming Christ-like, overlooks my faults. I count it a blessing to recognize that love, and a mercy that I'm blind to those faults. It doesn't matter that I'm not perfect—I don't have to be perfect to shine that good light—the imperfections keep me humble, human, and approachable, not too intimidating for those brothers and sisters still stumbling around in the dark.

So here we are: bit by bit, in spite of my caution, the lessons I tried so hard to keep at the arm's length of intellectual understanding seeped quietly through and soaked into my heart. It's true: if you willingly get Christianity on your hands, you are eventually going to get Christ in your heart.

I still don't know what's become of my siblings: whether they've managed to find the Way out of the maze of our childhoods. I hope they're listening, and that they'll respond when He calls them.

All three of my children did, and they share the good truth with friends who don't know.

We're on that road together, my children and I, and now we're following Him to a new home. Not *that* Home, yet; but we've outgrown this one, and it's time to move on.

I can't wait to see where He leads us next.

The End

Made in the USA
San Bernardino, CA
21 August 2016